LISA HARPER

LIFE

An Obsessively Grateful, Undone by Jesus, Genuinely Happy, and Not Faking it Through the Hard Stuff Kind of

100-DAY DEVOTIONAL

B&H
PUBLISHING
NASHVILLE, TENNESSEE

Published by B&H Publishing Group
Nashville, Tennessee

Dewey Decimal Classification: 248.84
Subject Heading: CHRISTIAN LIFE / QUALITY OF
LIFE / DEVOTIONAL LITERATURE

Cover design and handlettering by Tim Green at FaceOut
Studio. Author photo by Amy Conner.

3 4 5 6 7 8 • 25 24 23 22 21

I dedicate this to my daughter, Melissa Price Harper, who is tangible, giggling, dancing, singing proof that our God is a Redeemer.

ACKNOWLEDGMENTS

I'm indebted to the entire team at B&H but none more so than my editor, Ashley Gorman, whose wit and wisdom is reflected on pretty much every page of this devotional!

CONTENTS

Day 1

WILL THE REAL HAPPY PLEASE STAND UP?

*Happy the poor in spirit—because theirs is
the reign of the heavens.* MATTHEW 5:3 YLT

———————

HERE'S THE DEAL: YOU are going to be introduced to some real-life stories you'll surely resonate with in this devotional, as well as some wildly embarrassing ones that I hope you haven't had to deal with personally! Which means, sometimes you'll be turning these pages thinking, *Mmm hmm, I totally get that.* While other times you'll probably be reading along thinking, *This chick ain't right!* and may even find yourself chuckling at the blooper reel chapters in my story. And I'm all for that. I mean it. *Sign me up.* If you know me at all, you know I'm all about experiencing joy with God and each other in this crazy beautiful journey we call life—in the small moments, the big moments, the quiet moments, the loud moments, the bright moments, the dark moments. You get it. In *all the life-moments.* However, by the time you're a few devos deep into this darling (I can say that since I didn't have anything to do with the design!) pink book, you may find yourself wondering, *Why is happiness such a major theme?*

So let's start somewhere *super*-original and cutting-edge. Yes, I'm talking about the modern and wildly innovative world-wonder known as the dictionary. Good old Webster defines happy as: *characterized by or indicative of pleasure, contentment, or joy.*[1]

Though definitions are helpful, my instincts tell me you probably didn't need one on the concept of *happy.* Why? Because you are already familiar with it. The word itself immediately conjures up idyllic images or memories in our minds, doesn't it? Like a toddler in overalls splashing through puddles while gleefully chasing a frog. Or a couple of kindergartners sitting elbow to elbow at a picnic table both wearing gap-toothed grins and holding slices of watermelon bigger than their heads. Or a bright-eyed cheerleader who's catapulted high in the air with her arms over her head in victory when the home team scores the winning touchdown. *Happy*. It sounds like fireworks, smells like roasted marshmallows, and feels like cannon-balling into a cold pool on a hot day, right?

What it does *not* seem to be, to some of us, is allowable for Christians. Surely *happy* is too based on our circumstances, too emotive, too . . . well, too *unspiritual* to be an appropriate and consistent state for Christ-followers, right?

Wrong.

Wildly, sadly, distorted-by-religious-Pharisees-for-far-too-long WRONG.

There are actually thirty-seven references to "happy" in the Old Testament and forty-eight in the New Testament. Did you know that there are more than 2,700 passages where terms related to happy—*gladness, merriment, pleasure, celebration, cheer, laughter, delight, jubilation* and *feasting*—are used?[2] In fact, the Psalms—the book smack-dab in the middle of the Bible and comprised of 150 Old Testament *songs*[3]—literally begins with the word *happy*! See for yourself:

> *Happy* are those who don't listen to the wicked, who don't go where sinners go, who don't do what evil people do. They love the LORD's teachings, and they think about those teachings day and night. They are strong, like a tree planted by a river. The tree produces fruit in season, and its leaves don't die. Everything they do will succeed. (Ps. 1:1–3 NCV, emphasis mine)

While most of the translations of the Bible render this term as *blessed*—which admittedly has a more old-school, shiny wooden pew ring to it—super-smart scholarly people who are familiar with the grammar and syntax of original biblical manuscripts (folks like the awesome professors at Denver Seminary who are currently half-dragging me up the steep hill of their doctoral program!) assure us that the term *happy* is every bit as correct![4]

And let's not stop at the Psalms. Let's talk about how Jesus Himself used the concept of "happy." We don't have to look any further than the Beatitudes—arguably Jesus' most beloved message—which could accurately be titled "How to Be Happy" since the whole thing technically begins with the word *happy* as well. Once again, theological experts who've immersed themselves in the Hebrew, Greek, and Aramaic of biblical lexicon assert that "happy" (which in scriptural context is about the consistent joy that comes with trusting in God's faithfulness as opposed to the momentary enjoyment of present circumstances) is a perfectly sound substitutional term for "blessed" or "fortunate" here.[5]

That means *happy* is a wonderfully legitimate outward sign of Christians who are walking with God and enjoying all the inward graces He gives us. In other words, happiness is the joyful fruit of someone who is deeply rooted in their relationship with God . . . it's the outer disposition of a God-lover's inward reality . . . a covenant "state of being" for His people. Of course, that doesn't mean we won't have hard days—frankly, Jesus proclaims that we *will* most assuredly have hard days (John 16:33), but He also assures us there's no need to worry because He'll be with us every step of the way! The bottom line is, happiness isn't silly or unspiritual for Christ-followers but is actually a sacred, celebratory, and I daresay *necessary* aspect of our walk of faith. Break out those party poppers, y'all—because happiness isn't simply a *possibility* for believers; it's God's lavish and oh-so-accessible gift to help us live and love well in a world that's often less than kind.

My sincere hope is that you'll find your spiritual happiness increasing as you flip through these pages. God has taught me so much in every moment of life—from the lowest valley to the highest pinnacle. And at this middle-aged point, when I look back and realize that I've lived more life than I have life left to enjoy, I can promise you that I've never experienced God's absence. Not once. Whether I was laughing so hard there were tears running down my face or grieving so deeply that I ran out of tears, I can trace His sovereign, steadfast compassion through every single season. I firmly believe you'll find our Creator-Redeemer to be perfectly faithful and compassionate in the highs and lows of your life, too. So let's dive into this devotional and run hard toward Jesus together, knowing we'll inevitably share some pratfalls and belly laughs along the way!

- **WHEN'S THE LAST** time someone described you as happy?

- **HAVE YOU EVER** thought about happiness as being a sacred thing, in both the hard and the good times? Why or why not?

- **HOW CAN YOUR** external disposition better reveal your internal relationship with God?

Day 2

LAUGHTER REALLY IS GOOD MEDICINE

May all those who seek you be happy and rejoice in you. PSALM 40:16 NET

———————

ONE OF MY DEAR friends, Sheila Walsh, and I were invited to walk the red carpet a few years ago for the premiere of another friend's movie. But don't picture the typical red-carpet events that you've seen on television or in magazines! Imagine more of a burgundy indoor/outdoor-polypropylene-floor-covering kind of thing taking place at a multiplex in the suburbs next to several fast-food restaurants. Suffice it to say, we were tickled before we even got there.

Sheila's husband, Barry, chauffeured us to the event since we weren't sure we could walk—much less drive—in our snug, fancy dresses. We parked at the edge of the lot so we'd have privacy to make any necessary hair and makeup adjustments before facing the swelling crowd of eight or nine people who'd gathered to meet us. While the place he parked was private, it was also (unbeknownst to us) next to a grassy median that was soggy from recent rain. You can probably pick up on where this story is going. When Sheila lifted her gold silk skirt and stepped gracefully out of the car onto the adjacent turf, her 4-inch heels were immediately sucked into the mud, rendering her flailing and stuck like a stork in quicksand.

I sprang into action, heroically yelling for her to hang on while I attempted to squeeze myself out of the backseat of Barry's claustrophobic, two-door sports car that was obviously designed by sadists. Two broken fingernails and one snagged sleeve later, I finally emerged to be Sheila's saving grace, but as soon as I grabbed her arm to pull her to dry land, the heels of my shoes pierced through the muck too, effectively pinning me in place right beside her. We grabbed each other frantically, like two sailors who know their ship is going down fast and realize they've missed the opportunity to jump overboard.

As we toppled over in an ungainly heap, I really had no option but to fall squarely on top of my more petite pal. After much futile slipping and sliding, we began laughing hysterically and momentarily lost the ability to stand, even had we been able to find some leverage. This is the point in the story when, from somewhere underneath me, Sheila squeaked, "Help me, I'm peeing and I can't stop!"

Our recent "peetastrophe" was an effective reminder that, whether we're braving a red carpet premiere night or an ordinary weekday morning, the ability to laugh at ourselves is a key component to personal happiness.

Sometimes God does it through funny moments we share with friends. Other times He does it through intimate moments shared only with Him. He even does it through hard situations, in moments we wouldn't expect. But regardless of how He does it, God promises laughter and joy to all of His kids, even the leaky ones!

- **WHEN IS THE** last time you laughed so hard, you leaked?

- **IN WHAT AREAS** of life could you stand to take things just a little less seriously?

- **AT WHAT POINT** in your own story have you seen God give you laughter as a means to bravely walk through a difficult situation?

WHEN YOUR SPIRITUAL TUTOR IS A TOILET

For I am persuaded that neither death nor life, nor angels nor rulers, nor things present nor things to come, nor powers, nor height nor depth, nor any other created thing will be able to separate us from the love of God that is in Christ Jesus our Lord. ROMANS 8:38–39

INDOOR PLUMBING WAS A luxury in the Haitian village where my adopted daughter, Missy (full name Melissa), grew up. And soft, two-ply toilet paper? Even rarer. So, as you can imagine, when I finally brought her home to Tennessee, toilet flushing in our house with copious amounts of Charmin quickly became one of her favorite pastimes. Early on, as I observed the wide-eyed delight she displayed while watching massive plumes of paper spiral downward, my first thought was, "Isn't that just darling?" I wasn't even bothered when I had to call the plumber the first few times. But after a while, wading through ankle-deep wastewater in my bathroom (for some reason, she's partial to mine and has never once flooded the facilities in hers) and writing large checks to repairmen lost its allure.

I gave her cheerful lectures regarding the benefits of judicious toilet paper consumption. After that ceased to dissuade her from sending an entire forest down the drain during one particularly energetic (and unsupervised) potty episode, I grew more creative in my water-the-floor-no-more campaign and made up this catchy tune: "Five squares is where it's at, only moms need more'n 'dat. Tissue wads are so not cool, use single strips on the stool!"

Surely that would work, right?

Nope.

After various winsome strategies failed and my bathroom floors showed signs of warping, I employed more punitive consequences for her messy infractions. I limited iPad usage and confiscated one of her favorite Paw Patrol figurines. But nothing seemed to stem the tide.

Some months later, I was at my wit's end—to put it mildly—when I walked into my bathroom, past my innocent-looking daughter taking a bubble bath (she also likes my bathtub more than hers because it's bigger and "splashier"), and slipped on wet tile. It didn't take me long to discover water gushing out of the commode like Niagara Falls. After a heavy sigh I morphed into the put-upon persona my mother used when I did something especially naughty as a child:

Doggone it, Melissa, HOW MANY TIMES DO I HAVE TO TELL YOU that You. Do. Not. Use. Giant. Gobs. Of. Toilet. Paper. Like. This? Dadgummit, I. Am. So. Tired. Of. This, Missy! Why didn't you tell me you'd stopped up the toilet again and water was all over the floor?

The entire time I was plunging and fussing and mopping up that yucky pond with beach towels, I had my back to Missy. Within a minute or two—after my irritability had subsided enough to realize she hadn't responded to my questions—I turned around and was immediately convicted by the sight of my precious little girl sitting ramrod straight and staring at me mournfully as big tears streamed down her beautiful cheeks. I had all but crushed her spirit over something innocent and insignificant. She wasn't *trying* to cause a mess. She was still learning, still adjusting to a new life here. To having an indoor *toilet,* for crying out loud. She hadn't been willfully disobedient or disrespectful, so it wasn't a heart or character issue. It was a plumbing issue.

Losing my cool over something so minor prompted me to slide to my knees and thank God for being an altogether different kind of Dad. One who never turns His back on us despite our proclivity to make huge messes!

- **WHAT'S THE MESSIEST** thing you've done lately that our heavenly Father unexpectedly showed you grace and kindness over?

- **DID YOU REMEMBER** to thank Him for lavishing you with grace instead of lecturing you irritably?

- **WHO IN YOUR** life needs to hear that, because of Jesus, they don't need to fear God's anger over their messes? Are you living like this reality is true?

Day 4
NO MORE BARRIERS

When the angels had left them and returned to heaven, the shepherds said to one another, "Let's go straight to Bethlehem and see what has happened, which the Lord has made known to us." They hurried off and found both Mary and Joseph, and the baby who was lying in the manger. After seeing them, they reported the message they were told about this child, and all who heard it were amazed at what the shepherds said to them. But Mary was treasuring up all these things in her heart and meditating on them. LUKE 2:15–19

SINCE I FILLED YOU in on mine and Missy's adventure in potty training (and all the toilet paper that came with it), I may as well fill you in on April 14, 2014—another adventurous day in our history, and one I consider the second most important day in my life (second only to the day I met Jesus). Why? Because it's the day I brought Missy home from Haiti.

Because of Haiti's proximity to the US—it's only about a 90-minute flight from Miami—I had the privilege of visiting Missy multiple times during our two-year adoption process. Unlike some of my friends who've adopted from distant countries like China, Africa, or Russia, and didn't get to meet their kids until they traveled to their birth country to bring them home at the very end of the adoption process, Missy and I had the opportunity to spend two, three and even four days at a time together before our adoption was finalized. She'd even gotten into the habit of calling me "mama blan" (which means white mama in Creole), but since she associated me with short visits and presents, I think what she really meant by mama was "Santa with wider hips!" And since we had the blessing of establishing some semblance of relationship over the twenty-four months prior to April 14, 2014, I wasn't expecting such a huge shift to take place in my heart on our "Gotcha Day" (the day she actually came home to Tennessee). I mean, I knew that finally getting to bring her home was going to be *significant* . . . I just didn't know it was going to be *seismic*.

I can remember almost every detail of that day. The way she grabbed my hand and her eyes got really wide when the plane began to taxi toward takeoff in Port-au-Prince. The relief that washed over me when we stepped off the plane in Miami, on US soil for the first time. The way she giggled and wiggled in the long line at Customs. The peace that kept me grounded while it was taking so long for our paperwork to get processed in the Homeland Security and Immigration office that it looked like we were going to miss our connecting flight home to Nashville. The way she fell asleep on my lap once we finally made it on board and got settled into the back of that tiny plane. I can vividly remember the way we could hear our welcome home crowd cheering after we got off the plane in Nashville and began to walk toward baggage claim. We could hear them *long* before we could see them! I remember the way a famous country music star walking near us arrogantly assumed the boisterous crowd was cheering for him only to be shocked when they completely ignored him and his entourage because they only had eyes for a sweaty middle-aged mom and her newly adopted four-year-old.

But what I remember *most*—the memory that's the absolute highlight in an entire day of highlights—is the way I felt that first night at home, sitting on the bed next to her after she'd fallen asleep from sheer exhaustion. I remember being so overwhelmed with love for this little thirty-four-pound peanut that I had the literal, physical sensation of my chest expanding. The feelings of love and joy and gratitude and fulfillment were so big and so visceral, I felt like my ribs had to move over and make room.

I realized later that our first night at home was the first time there was no barrier between us. No reality that I had to leave her in the orphanage and fly back to America. No potential of yet another adoption delay. Nobody translating English to her or Creole to me. No lost Internet connection. Not even a dear friend holding a welcome sign or fervently praying. It was just the two of us. That's when the profound gift of parenthood matured from conceptual to concrete. From my longing for a child to a little girl under a Pottery Barn duvet whose eyelids fluttered while she dreamed and beautiful brown skin that smelled like cinnamon and coffee. Watching my daughter sleep that first night is among the purest, truest things I've ever experienced.

And Jesus' incarnation—when He left His celestial home and came to the world He created as God in the flesh—is infinitely better than that first night I experienced with Missy in our home. It's the moment the barrier between heaven and earth—between God and His people—dissipated. There in the wide-eyed wonder of a teenaged mom named Mary—who had a much more unconventional experience when it came to becoming a mom than I did!—we see the miracle of *God with us* begin to unfold.

- **DO YOU TEND** to be more of a concrete thinker or a creative processor?

- **HOW OFTEN DO** you ponder the miracle of an accessible Savior—that we can intimately know Jesus?

- **WHY DO YOU** sometimes forget that there's no barrier between you and God anymore? How might life be different for you if you approached God with the confidence that there are no more boundaries between the two of you, and that He delights over you, even as you sleep?

Day 5

REFUSE THE STARRING ROLE

For by the grace given to me, I tell everyone among you not to think of himself more highly than he should think. Instead, think sensibly, as God has distributed a measure of faith to each one. . . . Live in harmony with one another. Do not be proud; instead, associate with the humble. Do not be wise in your own estimation. ROMANS 12:3, 16

CAN WE ALL JUST agree that social media is rife with both blessings *and* difficulty? I once had the misfortune of wounding the pride of a female acquaintance when I neglected to give her the shout-out she felt she deserved on a certain social media platform. I only know this because, after noticing an effusive public post I'd made about another person I dearly love, she felt the need to share her disappointment with a mutual friend, who then shared it with me. Or, in short, you know, the grapevine. Mind you, I had called *and* texted personal congratulatory messages to the offended girl. But nonetheless, since I hadn't made the praise "public," she felt slighted. Sometimes I think pride masquerades as insecurity, which may be less offensive initially than a boisterous, noticeably big ego, but it's still fruit from the same self-focused tree. It's still all about us . . . it's just narcissism in a nicer outfit.

Speaking of being me-focused, I would be remiss if I made you think that gal is alone in her struggles. While mine isn't typically tricked out of hiding by perceived slights on social media, I've got my own nasty versions of self-centered insecurity and shame. And trust me, they definitely make themselves known on a regular basis! Like a few months ago when a Christian gentleman with whom I thought I had a real connection with on our first blind date never called again and told the person who'd set us up that he wasn't attracted to me, plus was put off by the fact that I came with the "baggage" of an HIV+ daughter. His barb not only sent me reeling to the dark chocolate cubby in the pantry, it convinced me to trudge down the path of self-pity. I wound up spending way too much emotional energy analyzing my unattractive parts (Missy not included—that joker was DEAD WRONG with that part of it. I may or may not have prayed for him to be trapped in a small room filled with hundreds of howler monkeys who were infected with irritable bowel syndrome for dismissing my baby girl as "baggage") and wondering what I could've done to be more alluring.

The bottom line is this: one less-than-flattering opinion about me from a balding man I only spent two hours with derailed my mind and heart from focusing on Jesus for at least ten times that many hours afterward. That's the real danger of pride-disguised-as-insecurity—it kidnaps us from living securely and abundantly based on the unconditional love Christ has lavished upon us, muffin top or not. And it embezzles time and energy we could've used to attend to lost and broken people around us. It bleeds us of the peace Jesus died to provide and it robs the world of the salt, light, and compassion His followers are called to provide. We weren't meant to spend time and mental energy and emotional output on how we stack up in the eyes of others, whether that be on social media or on a date or wherever it is for you. Instead of insecurity and pride, we all need to be reminded to instead pursue what St. Augustine called the three greatest characteristics of a Christian: "Humility, humility, humility."

- **WHEN DOES PRIDE-DISGUISED-AS-INSECURITY** tend to rear its ugly head in your life?

- **WHY DO YOU** think you struggle in this particular situation so often? What do you think is being taken from you?

- **WHAT DOES THE** pursuit of humility look like for you in this season of life?

Day 6

FIFTY-DOLLAR WORDS AND FIFTY-CENT FAITH

YOU MAY NOT KNOW this, but deep down, I'm a total nerd. I geek out on all things theological, which means it didn't take me long after undergrad to realize I'd probably *really, really* like seminary (schools for theology lovers). Now, don't get me wrong, I don't think this means I have to be a crusty old dinosaur hidden away in some basement library, away from real people and real-life issues. I like things down here in the real world, so I'm not planning on hiking up an ivory tower to set up shop any time soon!

Anyway, one of my favorite lecture series during my first seminary stint in a master's program was about having a "high view" of God. The main text our professor taught from was the following passage in Isaiah 6:1–8:

> In the year that King Uzziah died, I saw the Lord seated on a high and lofty throne, and the hem of his robe filled the temple. Seraphim were standing above him; they each had six wings: with two they covered their faces, with two they covered their feet, and with two they flew. And one called to another:
>
> > Holy, holy, holy is the LORD of Armies;
> > his glory fills the whole earth.
>
> The foundations of the doorways shook at the sound of their voices, and the temple was filled with smoke.
>
> Then I said:
>
> > Woe is me for I am ruined
> > because I am a man of unclean lips
> > and live among a people of unclean lips,
> > and because my eyes have seen the King, the LORD of
> > Armies.
>
> Then one of the seraphim flew to me, and in his hand was a glowing coal that he had taken from the altar with tongs. He touched my mouth with it and said:

Now that this has touched your lips,
your iniquity is removed
and your sin is atoned for.
Then I heard the voice of the Lord asking:
Who will I send?
Who will go for us?
I said:
Here I am. Send me.

You should have heard the lively discussions we had in class. The gist was this: in our quest to make the Gospel "relevant" to teenagers and unbelievers, we've all but lost the kind of awed reverence Isaiah displayed toward God. In our bumper-sticker-theology and God-is-my-copilot kind of culture, we've unwittingly minimized just how powerful and perfect and righteous the Alpha and Omega is. In our attempt to make Him more accessible, we sometimes lower our view of Him to nothing more than a buddy or self-help guru. I remember being convicted during that class that I didn't revere God the way I should. So I committed to be more careful in how I addressed Him in prayer and handled His Word. *I'm going to regard my Bible as a precious treasure instead of carelessly shoving it into a suitcase or tossing into the back seat of the car on a road trip. I'm going to give God the awe and respect He deserves!* And I still hold to those convictions.

However, as I look back over my walk of faith in the twenty years since then, it's clear that I sometimes overcorrected, ending up in the opposite ditch. In my sincere attempts to hold a high view of God, I made the mistake of assuming I had to hold a low view of myself. I began to teach Bible studies about "awe deprivation"—about the danger of having an anemic view of God. I also loved to quote the Latin phrase, *mysterium tremendum* (tremendous mystery), which I gleaned from one of my faith heroes, A. W. Tozer. In God's tremendous mystery, we should be confronted by God's greatness and in turn, be brought low. I also began weaving the word *depravity* into my testimony story, ensuring everyone knew I was saved purely by grace from a sinful pit I'd dug myself, and that I deserved death because of my transgressions.

It all sounded really lofty and academic to me at the time. And the truth is, a lot of that stuff isn't wrong. Sometimes we *do* have too casual a view of God. Sometimes we *should* stand in awe at God's mysteriousness. And we *are* saved by grace. But here's the problem: none of this means we should view ourselves as if God didn't delight in creating us! I didn't have the spiritual maturity back then to understand what I know now—namely, that having a truly high view of God *doesn't* result in having a low, degrading opinion of ourselves. Instead, having a high view of God opens the believer's heart and mind to what God says about us, His beloved children. Yes, apart from Him we're wicked and depraved, but after we put our faith and hope in Jesus Christ, we're allowed to shrug into His robes of righteousness and are adopted into the family of God as full heirs!

In Christ, our Father doesn't see us as worthless or dirty or depraved. He sees us as chosen, and righteous, and clean, and loved and a million other very happy things. Look in the mirror, friend. God wanted to save that person you see. He loves that person you see. He died for that person you see. If He has this loving view of you, why should you view yourself any differently?

- **WHERE WOULD YOU** put yourself on a "View of God" scale—with 1 being "I might believe in a higher power" and 10 being "I am so overjoyed by what Christ has done for me that I'm compelled to get on my knees and worship"?

- **WHERE WOULD YOU** put yourself on a "View of Self" scale—with 1 being self-hatred or narcissism and 10 being "I believe all the things God says about me are true!"?

- **IF YOU AREN'T** sure how God feels about you, what Christian in your life could you ask to help you be sure? On the flip side, if you're a Christian, who in your life needs reminding of how God truly feels about them?

Day 7

POSSUM-PROOF PEACE

Catch the foxes for us—
the little foxes that ruin the vineyards—
for our vineyards are in bloom. SONG OF SONGS 2:15

YOU MAY NOT KNOW that Missy and I live on what I like to call a "farmette"—a five-acre plot our log home is perched on (a.k.a.: Missy's Mountain). Anyway, not too long ago the winter sun had just set behind the snowy hill adjacent to the farmette, and I was musing contentedly about what a peaceful day we'd enjoyed. Missy was on the backside of a virus and although she no longer had a fever, she was still feeling a bit puny, so we stayed home in our pajamas—a lovely rarity for us—and watched family-friendly movies all day while the aroma of brownies baking permeated the whole house. I was merrily humming a tune from one of the old movies we'd watched when I took Maggie (the *very* energetic puppy I gave Missy for Christmas) outside for her final potty break of the evening.

But all that serenity was shattered when I was bombarded by a flash of fur and frenzied—albeit gleeful—barking. A possum had waddled out of the fringe of woods flanking our backyard, and our mischievous new pup took off after it like she'd been shot out of a cannon!

Of course, I was compelled to chase after both Missy's furry friend and the hissing, nasty looking marsupial to ensure that neither one of them got hurt in the melee. And thankfully, after much panting, hollering, and several ungainly slipping-and-falling-on-the-ice attempts, I was finally able to catch and carry a dramatically remorseful, squirming Maggie back up the steep hill to our house, allowing the possum to scurry back into the woods unscathed.

Maggie made it, thank goodness! However, I can't say the same for my pajamas. They got so mud-splattered in the process that I'm not sure they'll ever be wearable again and my favorite Ugg slippers now resemble days-old roadkill, complete with horse manure ground into the crevices of the soles!

I must confess in the midst of this possum debacle, I lamented not having a hunky, flannel-shirt-wearing husband—like some of the fictional dudes we'd just watched on the Hallmark Channel—to rescue me from all the dirty work our wee farmette requires. But after I opened the door and Missy realized it was actually her mommy and not some swamp monster under all that mud, gales of belly-laughter jerked me back into the glorious miracle of everyday life. Once I'd showered, changed into clean pajamas, and Maggie was snuggled up and snoring away in her crate, I sensed God whisper, "Do you really want to change this life I've lavished you with?" And I sheepishly whispered back, "No, Sir. No way!"

I mean, we all get a teensy bit frustrated about life's little inconveniences. But there's no way I'm going to let a possum take off with my peace again!

- **WHAT LITTLE FOXES** (a.k.a.: possums!) are threatening to steal the bloom of peace from your life?

- **HAVE YOU ASKED** God for wisdom regarding how to best send them scurrying back to the proverbial woods?

- **WHAT SPECIAL MOMENTS** or experiences jerk you back into the glorious miracle of everyday life?

GOOD GRIEF

You yourself have recorded my wanderings.
Put my tears in your bottle.
Are they not in your book?
Then my enemies will retreat on the day when I call.
This I know: God is for me. PSALM 56:8–9

IMAGINE IF A REALLY good, godly guy was just ambling along, minding his own well-behaved business when he fell into a deep pit of pain, loss, and suffering. Then, when he was buried up to his neck in misery at the bottom of that horrible hole, he found out God had supervised his terrible tumble! Surely that dude would renounce his faith in a compassionate Creator-Redeemer, right? Maybe get a huge, "God is dead or at least asleep at the wheel" tattoo across his back and choose Frank Sinatra's "My Way" as his go-to karaoke song for the rest of his post-pit life.

Well, that brow-raising scenario actually happened to a guy named Job and while history is blurry about the tattoo and karaoke bar parts (oftentimes the color commentary that runs through my brain is *not* biblically defensible!), it's crystal clear that Job didn't only retain his faith but his faith in the goodness of God *grew* exponentially.

A few of the top pit-takeaways from the Old Testament book of Job are:

- More often than not, the pain God allows into our lives isn't punitive but rather a promotion
- God's providence will never take us to a place where His grace won't sustain us
- We don't have to edit our emotions but can instead bring all of us to all of Him
- Grief is not the opposite of hope but rather proof of it

I resisted when God's Spirit initially prompted me to peruse the life of Job several years ago. Even though I'm a Bible teacher by passion and vocation,

I've done my best to avoid exegeting Job and assumed that to actually delve deeply into the text would be akin to sticking my hand in a blender. Or getting bamboo slivers jammed under my toenails. Or having my eyelashes pulled out one by one. Or listening to a telemarketer's entire spiel about the all-inclusive European vacation I'd won and simply needed to relay my credit card information to "reserve" the fabulous prize. You get the picture.

Anyway, after God's insistence that I befriend Job got too loud to ignore, I reluctantly began wading into his story and by the end of the first chapter, I was hooked. In fact, Job 1:20, which says: "Then Job stood up, tore his robe, and shaved his head. He fell to the ground and worshiped" has been a life-changer for me. Because the socio-historical context of Job tearing his robe and shaving his head means that he wasn't faking it—he wasn't wearing a happy face and pretending to be fine when his heart was eviscerated. He was *honest* with God about his ache. But he was also able to worship Him while he wept. This means that contrary to popular belief, confessing pain and expressing praise are not opposite ends of the "appropriate" behavioral scale for Christ-followers. Sometimes a hallelujah that's punctuated by a sob is actually sacred.

- **HAVE YOU EVER** experienced a broken heart and raised hands in worship at the same time?

- **IF NOT, ARE** you comfortable "letting" God see you cry?

- **IN WHAT WAYS** do you "fake it" before God? What could it look like—and feel like—to approach Him in total honesty instead?

Day 9
UNLIKELY FRIENDS

Jesus went up the mountain and summoned those he wanted, and they came to him. He appointed twelve, whom he also named apostles, to be with him, to send them out to preach, and to have authority to drive out demons. He appointed the Twelve: To Simon, he gave the name Peter; and to James the son of Zebedee, and to his brother John, he gave the name "Boanerges" (that is, "Sons of Thunder"); Andrew; Philip and Bartholomew; Matthew and Thomas; James the son of Alphaeus, and Thaddaeus; Simon the Zealot, and Judas Iscariot, who also betrayed him. MARK 3:13–19

WE ALL KNOW JESUS chose twelve disciples (which many say is His way of reconstituting, or at least nodding to, the twelve tribes of ancient Israel). I don't have the page space to go into great lengths about the diversity of this ancient fraternity that Jesus put together, but I do want to point out just two of the personalities that were forever merged together, though they once were completely irreconcilable.

Matthew the Tax Collector and Simon the Zealot.

Ever thought about how weird it is that the two of them were part of the same band of disciples? This Simon—not to be confused with Simon Peter—was a Jewish revolutionary who bitterly resented Rome's authority over Israel and the resulting persecution and oppressive taxation that came with it. In fact, Simon's hatred of Rome was so intense that prior to becoming a disciple of Christ, he'd been a card-carrying member of the Zealots. Who are the Zealots, you ask? An organization that endorsed extreme violence in its quest to overthrow Rome. And just to give you an idea of how radical the zealots were, they were known for hiding short, curved daggers in their cloaks and coming up behind Roman sympathizers in crowded marketplaces, jabbing them with the dagger in their back, and then jerking it upwards toward their heart. Which, of course, almost guaranteed immediate death. *Yikes.* Remember Barabas, the convicted murderer whose Passover pardon the crowd demanded from Pilate instead of Jesus? Well, Barabas was a contemporary of Simon the Zealot and killing a Roman sympathizer was the crime he'd been sent to prison for!

So you can imagine how shocking and humanly illogical it was for Jesus to plop Simon the Zealot nose-to-nose with Matthew the publican, who was paid by Rome to collect taxes on Jewish goods being imported and exported from Israel. This meant that Matthew had not only collaborated with Rome to extract unbearable taxes from his own flesh and blood, but according to historical records, he also likely skimmed off the top of those fees. He was in cahoots with the enemy, *and* lined his pockets with his own people's hard-earned money—money they truly couldn't afford to give away, and genuinely needed in order to feed their families! Before they encountered Jesus, Simon was jabbing people with daggers on one side of the political spectrum whereas on the other, Matthew was exploiting his hard-working friends and neighbors to beef up his personal bank account. (And these are *just two* of the disciples Jesus chose!)

You'd be hard-pressed to find two people more philosophically opposed than Matthew and Simon. A Rome-loving extortionist and a Rome-hating zealot. Putting them together was not unlike pairing Robert E. Lee with Ulysses S. Grant. Or an Alabama football fan with a Auburn football fan. Or a CrossFitter with a couch potato. Yet, in Christ, those two total opposites forged a brotherly bond. And that motley crew of men—apart from Judas, of course—became a cohesive group of missionaries. (We can only imagine the lively conversations they had traveling from town to town!) Their unlikely solidarity proves that the love of Christ can create deep relationships between former enemies. Or to borrow a line from Naomi and Wynonna who live right down the road from me, *Love can build a bridge!*

- **HOW HAS YOUR** relationship with Jesus helped you love people you didn't used to even like?

- **WHO IN YOUR** life do you consider the Matthew to your Simon? Who might you have massive differences with, but know you need to reconcile with because you are both Christians?

- **HOW CAN YOU** embody a brotherly or sisterly bond between you and someone you disagree with, whether politically or otherwise?

Day 10

MISSED AND MISUNDERSTOOD

From then on Jesus began to point out to his disciples that it was necessary for him to go to Jerusalem and suffer many things from the elders, chief priests, and scribes, be killed, and be raised the third day. Peter took him aside and began to rebuke him, "Oh no, Lord! This will never happen to you!" MATTHEW 16:21–22

ONE OF THE MOST heart-breaking habits I had to help Missy break during the first few months after she came home from Haiti was flinching. When I raised my hand to fix her bow or straighten her collar or caress her cheek, she'd recoil every time. It was obvious that much like Cookie, our gentle and loyal adopted dog who was beaten by her previous owner, Missy had received enough blows in her past to create deep-seated fear that surfaced whenever my hand got too close to her head or face. She soon learned enough English to express what she was feeling when she ducked; she'd say, "Mama, dat big lady at da or-pan-idge hit me wite heeaw" and point to her face. The first time she said it, I picked her up and held her for a long time, explaining softly over and over again that I would never, ever slap her in the face, hit her in the head, or intentionally hurt her. Once she finally relaxed and fell asleep in my arms, I laid her on the bed, pulled the covers up around her, walked outside of her room, leaned against the wall, and wept.

I'll never forget the look of terror that washed over Missy's face when she thought I was going to strike her. Or the angst of realizing that sometimes she was afraid of me. I mostly hated the abuse my baby girl had endured, which caused her to look at me in fear. But I also grieved that Missy didn't yet know the real me. And I can't help wondering since Jesus was incarnate—perfectly God *and* perfectly human—if He grieved the disciples' distorted view of Him, too. Their understanding of who He was obviously "mattered" to Jesus or He wouldn't have attempted to explain His death and resurrection to them multiple times, much less ask them, "But . . . who do you say that I am?" (Mark 8:29).

Do you think it's possible that He ached over being missed and misunderstood by His closest companions? Do you think it made Him sad or frustrated when people minimized His deity by essentially asking Him to perform tricks like a traveling magician (John 6:30–31)? Or how about when He was slandered, vilified, and set up for murder by the religious leaders of His day who made a living pouring over and preaching the Old Testament, which was *all about Him* (Luke 24:27)?

Years ago I was sitting in my counselor's office when she explained that one of the most common heartaches she hears is: *I just wish someone understood me.* She said the core of many of our emotional wounds is the pain of feeling missed or misunderstood. It broke my heart to be misunderstood by my little girl for just a few months . . . I can't begin to imagine the grief of being misunderstood by the entire world for whom you'd come to lay your life down for.

But the good news in all this is clear—in His death, burial, and resurrection, Jesus proved to the world exactly who He was. And He promises that He can not only empathize with us when we are misunderstood (Mark 8:21), but will one day make all of that right again, setting the record straight, and vindicating all those moments where someone got us wrong (Luke 8:17; Ps. 135:14).

- **THE BIBLE DESCRIBES** at least twenty distinct emotions that Jesus expressed—without sinning in the process—during His earthly ministry including: affection, anguish, anger, compassion, distress, grief, gladness, indignation, joy, love, peace, sadness, sympathy, agitation and exhaustion. Which of these are the most difficult for you to imagine Him feeling and/or expressing?

- **WHERE DO YOU** typically run for comfort when you feel misunderstood? How can you shift some things, and start running to God instead?

- **HOW DOES IT** help to know that you aren't alone in feeling misunderstood—that Jesus was misunderstood, too?

Day 11

A SEAT AT THE TABLE

David asked, "Is there anyone remaining from the family of Saul I can show kindness to for Jonathan's sake?" There was a servant of Saul's family named Ziba. They summoned him to David, and the king said to him, "Are you Ziba?" "I am your servant," he replied. So the king asked, "Is there anyone left of Saul's family that I can show the kindness of God to?" Ziba said to the king, "There is still Jonathan's son <u>who was injured in both feet</u>." 2 SAMUEL 9:1–3, EMPHASIS MINE

THE STORY BEHIND MEPHIBOSHETH'S limp is kind of like a Jerry Springer episode. I'm sure you remember he was the grandson of Saul, the first king of Israel, who was David's nemesis. But ironically, Saul's son and Bo's dad was a nice guy named Jonathan, who was David's BFF. The Bible tells us that Jonathan loved David as much as he loved himself. And Jon proved that when he defied his father to save David from certain death after hearing about Saul's plot to kill his homeboy (1 Sam. 20).

Years later, after both Saul and Jonathan were killed fighting the Philistines, and after many bloody battles between the house of David and the remnant of Saul's house, David finally won the right to occupy the throne of Israel. You may also remember from a world history class in high school that ancient kings were prone to murder the previous ruler's family members to thwart potential coups. Of course, David had no intention of following that tradition, but Saul's relatives didn't know that. And they were especially worried about the safety of five-year-old Mephibosheth, because he was the presumptive heir to Saul's throne. So they hurried to escape Jerusalem ahead of David's advance team. However, during their frantic departure, the nanny took a tumble with baby Bo, crippling him for life.

Now here we are twenty years later, and not long after David makes a nostalgic request in Jerusalem, one of his ambassadors knocks on Bo's door in *Lo-debar* (which means "barren place"). He shuffles to open it only to find a well-dressed official from Jerusalem standing on his stoop, who then asks him to gather his things and accompany him to the palace of King David. Surely Mephibosheth was terrified thinking, "What in the world does the king want with a cripple like me? Yikes, he must've finally decided to finish me off because granddad was such a jealous nutjob!"

> The king asked him, "Where is he?" Ziba answered the king, "You'll find him in Lo-debar at the house of Machir son of Ammiel." So King David had him brought from the house of Machir son of Ammiel in Lo-debar. Mephibosheth son of Jonathan son of Saul came to David, fell facedown, and paid homage. David said, "Mephibosheth!" "I am your servant," he replied. (2 Sam. 9:4–6)

Mephibosheth was physically scarred and emotionally marred. He was a scratch-and-dent kind of guy. He wasn't living the abundant life God promises; instead he'd limped to a barren place and had been languishing in that forgotten corner of the world for decades. Until a royal emissary knocked on his door and he assumed the jig was up. When Mephibosheth fell face down before King David, he probably didn't think he was going to be getting back up. He likely assumed the lethal stab of a sword was what was in store for him. Instead David does something unthinkable when compared to a typical king. Instead of having Bo killed or imprisoned because of his family history, David proclaims, *You will always eat meals at my table* (below in verse 7). This meant that Bo would now be enveloped into the royal family like a beloved, adopted son:

> "Don't be afraid," David said to him, "since I intend to show you kindness for the sake of your father Jonathan. I will restore to you all your grandfather Saul's fields, and you will always eat meals at my table." (2 Sam. 9:7)

David doesn't banish Bo from the earth, he invites him to his table. Similarly, we have been graced with an invitation to satiate ourselves with the scrumptious spiritual food at God's family table. Instead of being viewed as an enemy, we can now enjoy dining with Him and join in the welcoming conversation that wafts around the table like the aroma of fresh-baked bread. Because of all Christ did for us, no matter how debilitating our limp is or what our crazy backstory might be, the King bids us to leave the barren place and come home to a banqueting table laden with grace. To where we belong.

- **WHAT KIND OF** food would you choose to eat if you got to share a meal with a visible Jesus? Would you rather your first tangible dinner together be a formal or informal affair?

- **DO YOU EVER** consider yourself unworthy to come to God's table? How does this story encourage you?

- **WHO IN YOUR** life might need to hear that in Christ, they are welcome at God's table?

Day 12
AIRBORNE ATTITUDE ADJUSTMENT

Consider it a great joy, my brothers and sisters, whenever you experience various trials, because you know that the testing of your faith produces endurance. JAMES 1:2–3

— , • — —

SINCE MY JOB IS basically an itinerant evangelist, I'm typically on a plane two or three times a week. And over the years I've become a less-than-enthusiastic frequent flyer. I get tired of long security lines, canceled flights, and lost luggage, plus the fact that most plane seats are approximately the width of a supermodel's rear end!

Anyway, I was already a tad grumpy on a recent flight when I looked up and noticed an elderly woman loaded with bags boarding our motorized aluminum can. With jaded resignation, I sighed and thought, *I bet she sits next to me*, because even from twenty-five feet I could tell she was a talker.

Sure enough, after accidentally whacking me in the head with her purse, she wedged into the seat beside me and began chatting. I gave her a brief smile, then pointedly turned my attention back to the book I was reading so as to dissuade her from trying to make any more conversation. Instead, she perkily persisted in asking a litany of get-to-know-you questions. This caused me to muse to myself, "If I wasn't a Bible teacher, I would *so* lie right now and tell this woman I was a tax auditor who was tasked by the government to audit a randomly selected person on this very plane." That would surely create some distance.

Eventually my monosyllabic responses discouraged her into polite silence. I felt a twinge of guilt for shutting grandma down but before my guilt led to repentance, I fell asleep on my tray table. A little while later, I realized my iPod must've slid off the table, because I jerked awake while she was trying to carefully place it back next to my snoring face. And when I read the concern on her countenance, the seed of my earlier guilt blossomed into a mighty oak tree.

I sheepishly wiped the drool off my cheek and confessed, "I'm sorry I wasn't friendly earlier. I've just had a really hard week and am pretty tired. My name is Lisa, what's yours?" She smiled broadly and replied, "My name is Agnes and I'm eighty-three years old!" When I asked where she was going, she twisted to face me, arched both eyebrows with mischievous joy, and announced that she was headed to Mumbai, India!

I was taken aback that an eighty-three-year old woman was traveling halfway across the world by herself and exclaimed, "Wow! Why are you going to India, Miss Agnes?" She all but squealed in response, "I'm going to India to tell people about *JESUS!*" At which point I thought, *I'm going to be hit by a LIGHTNING BOLT for being such a grouch to such a dear saint!*

Agnes spent the next twenty minutes telling me her story. How she and her husband, Jim, were high school sweethearts who got married right after graduation and had their first baby when she was nineteen. How she put her hope in Jesus Christ soon after becoming a mom. Of course, she began praying that Jim would put his hope in the unconditional love of Jesus too and not only did he, but within a few years he became a pastor!

She said their life was blessed beyond her wildest dreams until they were in their mid-forties and Jim died in an accident. Shortly thereafter one of her grown sons died as well. Agnes said she thought her life was over. That she couldn't go on without her husband and son. But she said before she could "really get to wallowing," God spoke to her spirit and said, "Agnes, I'm the *love* of your life and Jim would want you to *get on* with your life!"

So she picked herself up and dusted herself off and decided to invest her heart into missions. With a twinkle in her eyes she enthused, "Lisa, I've been on fifty-one trips outside the US since then and I've never been more content. I've prayed with children in Africa and slept in a hut with a pastor's family in Mongolia. I've had the privilege of traveling all over the world to tell people about Jesus!"

After escorting my new friend to the international concourse, I had to run to catch my flight home to Nashville. But I wasn't grumpy anymore. Instead I grinned the whole way thinking to myself, *I want to be more like Agnes when I grow up! I want to live a pedal-to-the-metal, no-holds-barred, running-full-tilt-toward-Jesus kind of life!* May it be so of all of us—*even* if it takes some accidental narcolepsy and a purse-whack.

- **ON A SCALE** of 1 to 10—with 1 being "grumpy, pre-Agnes me" and 10 being "twinkly-eyed, world-changing Agnes"—where would you place yourself on a "counting it all joy" scale this season?

- **HOW HAS GOD** interrupted your life in an unexpected way, and reignited your passion for Him?

- **WHO IS A** spiritual Agnes in your life? What steps can you take to find someone like that to help you stay in a content-with-Jesus kind of place?

Day 13

THE UNDESERVED WITH-NESS OF JESUS

And you were dead in your trespasses and sins in which you previously walked according to the ways of this world, according to the ruler of the power of the air, the spirit now working in the disobedient. We too all previously lived among them in our fleshly desires, carrying out the inclinations of our flesh and thoughts, and we were by nature children under wrath as the others were also. But God, who is rich in mercy, because of his great love that he had for us, made us alive with Christ even though we were dead in trespasses. You are saved by grace! He also raised us up with him and seated us with him in the heavens in Christ Jesus, so that in the coming ages he might display the immeasurable riches of his grace through his kindness to us in Christ Jesus. For you are saved by grace through faith, and this is not from yourselves; it is God's gift—not from works, so that no one can boast. For we are his workmanship, created in Christ Jesus for good works, which God prepared ahead of time for us to do. EPHESIANS 2:1–10

LAST CHRISTMAS EVE, WAY out here in the hilly boonies of rural Middle Tennessee, Missy and I got to experience one of the most spectacular sunsets I've ever seen in all my fifty-six years. And I couldn't stop thinking about those ancient shepherds as I watched it. I kept picturing it—how soon after sunset in a small, Middle Eastern village 2,000+ years ago, they went from transient, very marginalized men with a reputation for petty thievery to VIP guests at the birth of the King of all kings. They were in fact the only guests invited to gape at Glory lying in a feeding trough that night. Also, fun fact: Contrary to the message sent by darling kids wearing their parents' bathrobes and pretend crowns dotted with fake gemstones during church Christmas pageants, the Wise Men didn't actually show up until Jesus was a toddler because of the extreme distance they had to travel on foot from Asia to Bethlehem!

Anyway, as I found myself watching the last tendrils of pink and orange slip below the horizon, and stars beginning to appear on the dark blue velvet canvas above us, I marveled again at how God's narrative—starting with lowly shepherds—makes it undeniably obvious that engaging with Jesus was never about our good reputation or laudable behavior. Jesus didn't rush to take selfies with the beautiful and popular mansion-dwellers while ignoring the poor and the powerless. Or, you know, those who could only count a few family members as their Instagram followers. Those shepherds, discombobulated by a supernatural star and immortalized in Luke chapter 2 (coupled with a super-long list of other Bible characters who received God's favor despite their considerable failures and frailty) underscore the mind-boggling truth that human connection with our Creator Redeemer is based on *His compassion,* not our *character.* I'll never get over the heavenly equation God saw fit to make a reality: faith in Jesus' work on our behalf + NOTHING we bring to the table to try and justify ourselves = salvation.

After we came inside to warm up by the fireplace and enjoy the twinkling lights of our Christmas tree, Missy asked why some people call Jesus *Immanuel.* I explained how that name was prophetically given to Him in the Old Testament and it literally means "God with us." Then I chuckled softly over how wildly blessed we are that His "with-ness" isn't determined by our deservedness. He is with us—shepherds to salesmen to scientists to stay-at-home moms—not because we did anything to make Him do it. But because He wants to be. Because He decided to be. Because He loves to be.

- **CONSIDER THE EQUATION:** faith in Jesus' work on our behalf + NOTHING we bring to the table to try and justify ourselves = salvation. What have you been guilty of bringing to the table to try and justify yourself with God?

- **HOW DOES IT** encourage you that Jesus chooses to be with you because He wants to be?

- **WHEN ARE YOU** most tempted to forget that God doesn't relate to you based on your good reputation or behavior? Whose good reputation and behavior does He see when He looks at you?

Day 14
JESUS DIDN'T SOCIAL DISTANCE

He went into all of Galilee, preaching in their synagogues and driving out
demons. Then a man with leprosy came to him and, on his knees, begged him, "If you
are willing, you can make me clean." <u>Moved with compassion</u>, Jesus reached out his
hand and touched him. "I am willing," he told him. "Be made clean." Immediately
the leprosy left him, and he was made clean. MARK 1:39–42, EMPHASIS MINE

THE SHORT STORY ABOVE is from Mark's Gospel account, and the "moved with compassion" part can also be translated as "moved with pity" or "felt sorry for the man." This phrase, however your Bible translation renders it, comes from one word in the original Greek text: *splangnitzomai*. Sounds like a pasta, no? Well, that pasta-sounding word comes from somewhere too, namely, the root word *splanchnon*, which sounds like an organ, right? Indeed! This is where we get the English word *spleen* from—and it was also used in ancient texts when referring to the bowels or innards or a person. *Innards*. What a word.

Okay, so what's the point of this Greek vocabulary lesson that I'm sure you woke up today dying to have? Mark's big point is that the compassion Jesus extended to the leper came from His *guts*. From the innermost core of Jesus Christ. In other words, when He encountered this disfigured man outside the city gates, Jesus didn't think to himself, "Wowzers, that's one nasty case of leprosy. Poor guy better get himself to a good dermatologist!" Our Savior didn't simply toss a little superficial concern in the leper's general direction. "I'll pray for you, man!" No. Jesus experienced deep, visceral, compassion for him.

The kind of gut-level kindness we observe here in Jesus is especially significant when you consider how leprosy was viewed in the first century. Not only was it a devastating, potentially fatal disease (and highly contagious), it also poisoned its carriers with crippling social stigma. In fact, according to Old Testament law, lepers had to walk around in ripped clothes and unkempt hair yelling, "Unclean, unclean!" whenever they were in public places. Why? So no one would approach them and possibly become contaminated themselves (Lev. 13:45). They were also commanded to live alone. That means this poor guy in Mark 1 was an utter pariah. He'd likely lost contact with his family, had no friends outside of the leper colony, and hadn't experienced the touch—or maybe even the eye contact—of another human being in years.

In light of his hideous deformities and the stigmatization that came with being ceremonially unclean, it would've made sense for Jesus to keep His distance. To just wave His hand and heal the guy without any physical contact. Instead, our tenderhearted Savior reaches out and touches the man *before* healing his diseased body. The guy isn't healed yet, and Jesus intentionally makes physical contact. His gesture implies, "I won't just love you on the other side of this physical ailment, once you're clean and whole again. I love you now, right in the middle of it. Right in the place where you feel unseen or unloved or dirty. You *matter* to me." He was not only interested in healing the man physically, but relationally too—bringing him from isolation to community, from shame to security.

This miracle illustrates that the heart of God is moved by the wounds of humanity. Our ache accelerates His compassion. He intentionally reaches out to restore us when we find ourselves filthy and ashamed before him. May we always trust God's gut.

- **DO YOU TEND** to try to "clean yourself up" before approaching Jesus? Or are you comfortable leaning into His love when you're still "dirty" feeling disfigured or ashamed?

- **HOW DOES IT** feel to know that Jesus intentionally reaches toward you, even when you're still in the middle of your wounds?

- **WHO IN YOUR** life is a social outcast? Following in Jesus' example, how might you draw near to them and love them right in the middle of their difficulty or dysfunction?

Day 15

WHEN THE SLIPPER DOESN'T FIT

I adorned you with jewelry, putting bracelets on your wrists and a necklace around your neck. I put a ring in your nose, earrings on your ears, and a beautiful crown on your head. So you were adorned with gold and silver, and your clothing was made of fine linen, silk, and embroidered cloth. You ate fine flour, honey, and oil. You became extremely beautiful and attained royalty. Your fame spread among the nations because of your beauty, for it was perfect through my splendor, which I had bestowed on you. This is the declaration of the Lord GOD. EZEKIEL 16:11–14

I WAS CHATTING WITH a Southern belle friend of mine recently over coffee about the concept of human depravity—about how our ships are so totally sunk apart from the transformational power of God's grace. After a while, she sighed heavily and then mused dreamily, "The Gospel reminds me of the Cinderella story." She went on to explain how she thought humanity was like Cinderella, and Jesus was like the divine prince.

I don't remember how I responded verbatim; I think I just hemmed and hawed a bit and then changed the subject. But her innocent observation rubbed the fur of my heart in the wrong direction and I kept mulling over it after we said goodbye . . . until eventually the source of my angst hit me.

Here's the deal: if you've read the book or rented the movie, you know that Cinderella *deserved* the prince. She was gorgeous, she was personable, she had a strong work ethic, and she was kind to animals (who in their right mind is nice to mice living in their clothes and bed and eating all their hard-earned Gouda cheese?). Not to mention that *voice*. Furthermore, the fact that she was used and abused by her soap-opera version of a stepfamily made her a very sympathetic character. So when the glass slipper fits and the fairytale concludes with happily ever after, we can turn the proverbial page with happy satisfaction because good triumphed over evil and sweet Cindy earned the title of princess, right?

But that's not at all what happens in the Gospel. In God's *true* story, the ugly, horrible, abusive stepsister gets to marry King Jesus. He picks the chick wearing that hideous, wide-striped polyester dress. The awkward, snarky girl with a huge, hairy mole on her chin. Not to mention her self-centered heart. I mean, come on. She's the girl who locked her sister in a tower in order to get ahead! She's horrible to animals! And she can't sing a note! Everyone at the ball is dumbfounded when he gallantly strides across the dance floor, extends his hand and asks *her* to join him for the waltz. I can just hear the ladies muffling under their breath to each other, behind their fans. *Um, looks like the royals have seriously lowered their standards.* But right there, in front of that shell-shocked crowd, the ugly stepsister *becomes* beautiful in the adoring, undeserved gaze of the handsome prince. It's not a fairy godmother who bedecks her. It's the Prince. *His* love transforms her—and not just with a designer outfit. But from the inside out. The Prince transforms her into everything we thought she could never be. He takes her record of selfishness (and almost unforgivable tone-deafness) and pays for it himself, and then clothes her in honor and splendor. She didn't earn a thing!

That's the divine love story we've been written into. We were once the ugly stepsister, you and me. That's who we were. But now we're royalty. That's who we are now. All made possible by the One, true, perfectly and powerful King who picked the worst of us out of a crowd and made us His very own.

- **IF YOU COULD** actually see Jesus gazing at you with undisguised affection, do you think you'd bask in His love or look away?

- **WHY IS IT** a little offensive, at first, to consider yourself as the stepsister in this scenario? Why is it also a little freeing?

- **YOU KNOW JESUS** saved you, but do you also believe He can transform you—even now? What makes you forget this sometimes?

Day 16
GOOD FRIDAY WAS PREMEDITATED

"Fellow Israelites, listen to these words: This Jesus of Nazareth was a man attested to you by God with miracles, wonders, and signs that God did among you through him, just as you yourselves know. Though he was delivered up according to God's determined plan and foreknowledge, you used lawless people to nail him to a cross and kill him. God raised him up, ending the pains of death, because it was not possible for him to be held by death." ACTS 2:22–24, EMPHASIS MINE

WHEN I WAS IN middle school, I went to a youth rally in Orlando where I heard an energetic and engaging youth pastor tell a story that haunted me for a long time. It went something like this:

Once upon a time there was a very kind man who lived in quaint log cabin in a remote area of the Great White North with his lovely wife and beloved son, who'd been born to them after over a decade of infertility. The man made an honest living operating a drawbridge that allowed twice daily commuter trains to pass safely over a large lake in the mountains where they lived.

The drawbridge operator's little boy was both his namesake and the apple of his eye, so it delighted him when Junior accompanied him to work every Saturday. He often let him sit on his lap and push the button to lower the drawbridge and then wave cheerfully at the train passengers whizzing past the control booth on their way to the big city. But one Saturday Junior brought a bright red ball to entertain himself with and moments before the afternoon train rolled through, the ball rolled away from him down the hill and came to rest on the tracks below.

The train's whistle drowned out the father's bellowed warning not to chase after the ball, and his heart dropped as he saw the train racing around the bend at the exact moment his boy took off toward the ball. He had a split second to choose whether to leave the control booth and rescue his child, thereby condemning hundreds of commuters to their death by not lowering the drawbridge, or he could sit tight in the booth and do his job, thereby saving hundreds of strangers yet crushing his only son in the process.

He instinctively chose the latter. And then sat in stunned horror while hundreds of oblivious men, women, and children hurtled past with hands raised in happy greeting.

When the youth pastor got to the end of the story he added soberly, "And that's exactly what God did for every single one of us. He crushed Jesus, His only begotten Son, to rescue you." Of course, there was a huge altar call response that night as hundreds of kids—including myself—tearfully raced to the front of the arena, burdened with fresh guilt over the fact that because of our reprehensible behavior, God panicked and hit some dreadful button in heaven that condemned dear Jesus to death on a cross. Most of my girlfriends and I wept bitterly all the way home in an old fifteen-passenger church van, while the boys stared mournfully out the window at flickering interstate billboards because this was an era before hand-held high-tech devices, not long after all the dinosaurs died.

For years afterwards, I wondered and worried about that drawbridge operator and his wife. I thought about how hard Christmas morning must be with their son's stocking missing from the mantel. How bleak his birthday must be now for them to endure without him every year. How that father must be in continual torment over whether or not he made the right choice. It wasn't until decades later during a seminary class that I found out the train story was a complete fabrication. It never actually happened. It's the spiritual edition of an urban legend and was conjured up by some creative, albeit manipulative, soul as an illustrative "tool" to help people recognize the magnitude of their sin.

I'm not saying illustrations or old wives' tales or legends can't be used in a sermon, because I've heard many pastors, preachers, and Bible teachers use them with responsible efficacy. But here's the deal: there is no anguished operator in some ethereal drawbridge booth. The Creator of the Universe *planned* every detail of divine redemption. God chose the nails that would be driven into His boy's wrists and feet and grew the trees that would sprout the thorns, which would eventually be woven into a mock crown and cruelly jammed onto His precious, only child's head. Our Savior's death was not a knee-jerk reaction; it was a carefully and divinely orchestrated mission of mercy.

And on top of that, let's just be clear: Jesus didn't accidentally stumble onto the cross trying to chase a ball. He *chose* to go there. It's the whole reason He came to earth in the first place. He showed up to the tracks with the ropes, as it were, ready to tie Himself to them if He had to. He *willingly* laid His life down (John 10:17–28). Yes, the Father sent Him, but at the same time, Jesus also volunteered. The Father's finger pointed for Him to go, as if to say, "you will be the one to do it," at the *very same moment* His Son's hand went up in the air to say, "I want to do it. Please let Me do it." They were in perfect agreement. Though it would require such pain and agony, in the end, it was the Father's joy to make a way for you and me to be saved, just as it was a joy for Christ to *be* that Way (Isa. 53:10; Heb. 12:2).

So, rest assured, friend. The cross wasn't a sudden shock on the Father's part, nor an accidental horror story (or a forced fate) on the Son's. It was chosen in joy by them both. You can believe that today.

- **HOW DOES IT** make you feel that Jesus joyfully endured the cross for YOU?

- **WHAT MISCONCEPTIONS ABOUT** Jesus' work on the cross have weighed you down in guilt?

- **DID YOU KNOW** that the Father and Son agreed on the plan of the Gospel—if not, how does this help you process what happened on the cross?

Day 17
A LITTLE RAIN WON'T HURT YA

"For he causes his sun to rise on the evil and the good, and sends rain on the righteous and the unrighteous." MATTHEW 5:45

NOT LONG AGO, MISSY and I had a posterior-numbing twelve-hour road trip returning home from a wonderful women's conference in south Alabama. Of course, it should've only been seven hours, but we made one rather lengthy pit stop in Troy, Alabama, to eat at Crowe's (which has been serving the *best* fried chicken since I went to undergrad at Troy University 30+ years ago!). Oh, and I was also not letting my polite—albeit completely unimpressed—child get out of this trip without walking around Troy's campus in the drizzling rain while I shrieked things like, "Baby, this is the cafeteria where we ate our meals when I was in school here!" and "Miss, see that old building behind those magnolia trees? That's the gym where I played college volleyball!" and "Honey, that pond over there is where I got dunked when I pledged Kappa Delta!" Parental bragging rights, you see.

And I guess all that happy reminiscing sapped my common sense just like leaving your car lights on drains your battery. How so, you ask? Well, wouldn't you know that when we pulled into our driveway in Tennessee many hours later, my wallet wasn't with us? I had accidentally left it in a gas station at our last pit stop.

Of course, I didn't notice it was missing until the next morning when I picked up my purse before heading out the door and thought, *Wow, this sure is light.* Then I got that pit in my stomach—you know how it feels—when I began rummaging around in said purse and couldn't find said wallet, realizing it could be at *any one* of the three or four potty/coffee/gas stops we made in Alabama and Tennessee on the way home. It took thirty minutes of retracing my steps and frustrating phone calls before finally discovering where I'd left it. Then, while talking to the manager at the store I'd left it in, it became apparent that whoever had graciously turned it in had also ungraciously rifled through it and taken the $400 cash that was in it first!

I know being "robbed" of four hundred dollars from a wallet I'd left in a bathroom stall in the middle of nowhere was *totally* my fault, but I still felt somewhat deflated when Missy and I got in the car to drive all the way back there to reclaim it. I thought, *Ugh, I've got a million things to do, the last thing I need is to spend half the day chasing down my wallet and feeling guilty about losing four hundred hard-earned bucks.* After driving in silence for a few minutes, Missy asked me if I was sad. I said, "Just a little bit, baby." When she asked why, I explained that someone had taken our money without asking.

Which left both of us feeling a little subdued when we stopped to get sub sandwiches a few minutes later to eat on our wallet-retrieval-road-trip. But then, right as I was pulling money out of my pocket (since I was still sans wallet!) to pay for our lunch, a woman—whom I'd already noticed when we walked in because she was grinning from ear-to-ear—stepped in front of me and swiped her credit card to pay for our food! She laughed at my momentary bewilderment and went on to explain that she'd been really encouraged by my Bible studies and was tickled to meet Missy and me. She said buying our lunch was the least she could do to thank us for the spiritual blessing we'd brought into her life! While I was busy focusing on that stranger who stole without permission, God was divinely orchestrating another stranger to drop in our lives; one who would *bless* without permission.

I couldn't stop smiling as we rode down the interstate happily snacking on free subs en route to pick up my mostly empty wallet (thankfully the wallet returner/cash thief had chosen to leave my driver's license and credit cards). When Missy asked sincerely, "Mama, was that lady at Firehouse Subs an angel?" I couldn't help laughing before replying, "Maybe, baby. Maybe."

After my teensy First World problem was turned on its head by a generous sub-shop cherub, I also couldn't help musing, "Instead of focusing on the inevitable rain in life, I want to focus on the inevitable sunshine." Because in view of our perfect heavenly Father, who gives good gifts to His children, even our deepest disappointments will ultimately prove to be gatekeepers for future delight. No matter how hard it's raining in our lives now, it's really only a thimbleful of liquid in the vast ocean of God's sovereignty. And may we never forget that in the divine template of eternity, *this too shall pass.*

- **WOULD YOU DESCRIBE** your life as having more rainy days or sunshiny ones?

- **WHEN HAS GOD** surprised you with a needed blessing—one you didn't see coming?

- **HOW HAVE YOU** seen God turn a rainy season into something beautiful?

Day 18
LEARNING TO LINGER

Therefore we do not give up. Even though our outer person is being destroyed, our inner person is being renewed day by day. For our momentary light affliction is producing for us an absolutely incomparable eternal weight of glory. So we do not focus on what is seen, but on what is unseen. For what is seen is temporary, but what is unseen is eternal. 2 CORINTHIANS 4:16–18

——

WHEN IT COMES TO rest and implementing a practical Sabbath—actually carving out at least one full day each week to worship God and allow Him to replenish my body, mind, and spirit—I'm a slow learner. Worse still, sometimes I'm willfully disobedient. Stillness has never come easy for me. Running on fumes does, but not rest.

Mind you, some of my go-go-go is hardwired in my personality and some of it has to do with my calling. I mean, it's pretty hard not to be passionate and raring to run as fast as you can when your "job" involves seeing people put their hope in the unconditional love of Jesus Christ, prodigals returning home, relationships restored, and formerly dead bones getting down on the dance floor!

However, much of my burn-the-candle-at-both-ends mindset is tied to shame. I do understand cognitively that God doesn't love me any less if I'm sitting on a beach instead of sharing the Gospel, investing in a missional cause, or cleaning the baseboards. And the sovereignty of our Creator-Redeemer is part of what I love most about God and is just so central to my theology, so I don't for a moment really think He "needs" me to accomplish His will. But there's still a small, bruised corner of my soul secretly clinging to the idea that my worth and productivity are inextricably linked. That I'm only precious in His sight when I'm getting something done.

Thankfully, the Lord's kindness is unchanging, and He is committed to creatively teaching me why resting in Him is the better way, every single time. For example, He has recently taught me this through little moments with Missy—moments I would have missed if I was in a hurry. Like when I heard her happy giggle preceding her body down a giant, curlicue slide, or saw her face filled with joyful abandon when she raced around the yard with our dogs Cookie and Maggie, or felt her warm hand clasp mine when we lazily ambled down our long driveway to check the mailbox. When I took the time and gave myself the margin to notice, I realized I was filled to the brim with delight and contentment over Missy simply having fun. In those sweet moments, I could sense our heavenly Father whispering, "Those huge waves of love you feel for your daughter are mere drops compared to the ocean of affection I have for you." As you can imagine, I smiled gratefully, renewed in my commitment to linger in His embrace longer and not wriggle out of His presence the first chance I get in some unnecessary attempt to "earn my keep."

That's what Sabbath does for us all—it helps us stay still long enough to bask in just how much He delights in us. If we spend all of our days in a hurry, we'll miss that. And I don't know about you, but whether I'm chasing a dog around a yard or curling up with a blanket and His Word, I need to remember that this is how God feels about me. Frankly, I think we all need the reminder that He is filled to the brim with contentment and delight over us, and to let His overflow fill us up.

- **ON A SCALE** of 1 to 10, with 1 being "burn the candle at both ends" and 10 being "total couch potato," where would you place yourself?

- **DO YOU THINK** spiritual rest always requires us to cease physical activity? Why or why not?

- **IN WHAT WAYS** do you try to "wriggle free" from God's presence? What steps could you take to linger a little longer?

Day 19

SKIN IN THE GAME

*Then he said to them all, "If anyone wants to follow after me, let him deny himself,
take up his cross daily, and follow me. For whoever wants to save his life will
lose it, but whoever loses his life because of me will save it."* LUKE 9:23–24

AFTER I BEGAN THE process of adopting Missy, who is from Haiti, someone sent me a couple of really cool "Pray for Haiti" baseball T-shirts. I loved wearing those T-shirts because they inevitably led to conversations with people in Starbucks about how it was our Christian *responsibility* in a First World context to help oppressed people groups in Third World countries. These people make less in a day than we Americans spend on a cup of fancy coffee—how in the world can we withhold the blessings God has given us when we know this? I usually walked away from those impassioned chats in my hipster Haiti T-shirt feeling pretty darn good about myself.

But then my friend Tracie invited me to join her and volunteer for a medical mission trip, which would actually work out perfectly, as the trip was scheduled a few days before my and Missy's next planned visit in Haiti. As God would have it, this service-oriented mission dovetailed perfectly with my calendar.

Since I have no medical experience—I literally wrote "lifting heavy things and verbal encouragement" in the blank on the form where we were supposed to describe any useful skills we had that pertained to the project—I ended up being assigned to assist a nurse in the "Scabies Clinic." This, of course, meant I stood in 110-degree heat in an outdoor pavilion under a tin roof and washed, then applied antibiotic ointment to a seemingly endless line of men, women, children, and infants whose skin was infested by scabies.

If you aren't familiar with scabies, it's a highly contagious, communicable disease caused when mites—sometimes referred to as body lice—burrow under human skin. Which of course causes manic itching, which leads to open sores, which can lead to much more serious, opportunistic infections and illness, especially in babies and children already suffering in impoverished conditions. And because little kids and infants who are suffering from scabies are typically fussy because they're so miserable, I ended up cuddling most of them so they'd trust me enough to wash their wounds and cover their "owies" with cream.

It was easy to prance around in a "Pray for Haiti" T-shirt in an air-conditioned coffee shop in Middle Tennessee, but it wasn't quite so easy to seal it (and all the other clothes I brought back from Haiti) in a plastic bag and burn it because I'd come home itchy and infected, too. We all need reminders that there is a huge difference between coaching from the spiritual sidelines and putting skin in the game. Between advertising for the cause and actually joining it. Between talking about it from afar and getting close enough for it to affect our comfort. God may not teach you this through a Scabies Clinic like He did me, but I wonder, how might He be trying to teach you this very thing in your own context?

- **WHERE ARE YOU** sacrificing time, money, and energy for the sake of the Gospel?

- **ON A SCALE** of 1–10, with 1 being "sitting unconcerned on the sidelines" and 10 being "wearing a jersey covered in blood, sweat, and tears," how invested are you in being the hands and feet of Jesus Christ to a lost and broken world?

- **WHAT MINISTRY OR** cause might God be calling you to get close enough for discomfort?

Day 20
SHOO FLY, SHOO

Finally brothers and sisters, whatever is true, whatever is honorable, whatever is just, whatever is pure, whatever is lovely, whatever is commendable—if there is any moral excellence and if there is anything praiseworthy—dwell on these things. PHILIPPIANS 4:8

A FEW YEARS AGO I was carpooling to a social event with a few friends and acquaintances, and one of them kept complaining the entire trip. I didn't know her well but had heard she was a bit of a negative Nancy, so after a while, I just joined in with the other girls and mumbled non-committal "mmm hmmms" to her whiny and exhausting glass-is-just-*so-so-so*-half-empty declarations.

If the traffic doesn't thin out, we're going to be late. Mmm. Hmmm.

If that car in the next lane gets any closer, he's going to ram us. Mmm. Hmmm.

If it gets any hotter, I'm going to break out in a heat rash. Mmm. Hmmm.

If they don't have lactose-free options tonight, I'm either going to starve or have terrible gas. Mmm. Hmmm.

If the stock market gets any more volatile, there will be a global financial crisis. Mmm. Hmmm.

If she swerves again, I'm going to throw up—

This was the point where I couldn't take her Eeyore-isms any longer, so I said something along the lines of, "Mind over matter usually works for me, so maybe if you don't think about being carsick you won't feel nauseous." I even said it with a smile. But I may as well have said, "You are a horrible creature with a really big bottom and we're all wishing we could pull over and dump you out on the side of the interstate right about now because you're getting on our collective last nerve." Because she gave me a withering look and then retorted snidely, "Well, excuse me, Lisa, but I wasn't born all *happy-go-lucky* like you."

I *so* wanted to snap back, "Baby, my happy has *nothing* to do with luck. I've worked my tail off for this joy!" However, I didn't want to risk being punched in the nose, so I just thought it very quietly to myself.

The truth is, no one's happiness is based on luck if their joy is genuine. Happy is not the result of happenstance. It's not a fluke or an accident nor is it largely dependent on our circumstances. And, as it turns out, this isn't just something the Bible shows us. Science agrees, too! Research reveals that only 10 percent of our happiness is connected to our circumstances, 50 percent of it is linked to genetic factors and temperament, and the other 40 percent is entirely within our control because it's determined by our choices, thoughts, and behavior.[6]

Did you get that? ALMOST HALF OF THE DETERMINING FACTORS FOR HAPPINESS ARE REGULATED BY ME AND YOU! Goodnight, y'all . . . that means even if your hair is chemically dependent, your metabolism has slowed to a crawl, and your online dating algorithms are all whacked out and you keep being matched with men who are unemployed and live in their mother's basement (I'm just going out on a limb here and speaking metaphorically, of course), you can still *choose* to be joyful! Our thought-life doesn't have to be the boss of us!

Frankly, if we've put our hope in Jesus Christ, our thought-life is under the authority of the Holy Spirit. That doesn't mean every single thing that sails through that space between our ears will be sacred, but listen, *we don't have to be controlled by pessimism, cynicism, or fear* either! As the old adage says: "You can't stop the birds from flying over your head, but you can keep them from making a nest in your hair."

- **WOULD YOUR FRIENDS** and family describe you as a glass-is-half-full or glass-is-half-empty kind of person?

- **WHAT MOST TEMPTS** you to focus on the negative things? How does it encourage you to know that being happy is actually well within your own control?

- **HOW COULD YOUR** life look different if your words and thoughts focused primarily on "whatever is true, whatever is honorable, whatever is just, whatever is pure, whatever is lovely, whatever is commendable"?

Day 21

THE SILVER SPOON OF SALVATION

What, then, are we to say about these things? If God is for us, who is against us? He did not even spare his own Son but gave him up for us all. How will he not also with him grant us everything? ROMANS 8:31–32

———

ALL TOO OFTEN CHRISTIANS proclaim on the belief-level that "Jesus is all we need," yet in practice, our behavior clearly says, "We have to take care of ourselves." For example, we anxiously fill in all our Bible study blanks not because we long to know Jesus more intimately, but because we're afraid if we don't check off every item on our spiritual to-do list, then God will be disappointed in us. Surely, slothful Bible study habits will lead to a government-subsidized apartment in heaven instead of the mansion our Messiah promised, right? We believe the truth, but sometimes *live* in a lie: *Jesus made the way for me, yes, but it's all on me to keep things that way!*

If only we could grasp the fact that we're God's beloved heirs and no longer orphans.

When mealtime came during my visits with Missy at the orphanage in Haiti, she'd grab my hand and urgently pull me toward the food table with her head held high and a huge grin spread across her face. Because when she was with me, her *mama blan*, the nannies wouldn't turn her away from the table. My watchful presence ensured her plastic plate would be pilled high with everything she pointed to. Rice: overflowing spoonfuls; chicken legs: all the drumsticks she could eat; bread: at least three pieces; mango: unlimited slices! My little girl learned quickly that when the large, pale American lady was by her side, she didn't have to beg or subsist on a bowl of watery porridge.

Oh how much sweeter the nepotism is with our heavenly Father and His kids! God is so eternally committed to caring for us that He sent His only begotten Son to establish a *new way* of coming to the table. Instead of trying to balance our hefty hopes on the slender shoulders of one flawed human priest, we get to place them on the infinitely broad back of the Prince of Peace. Jesus accomplished our reconciliation with God forever through His death and resurrection. His sacrifice on the cross shredded the curtain that separated sinners from a holy God. His blood washed away the stain of sin and the stigma of shame, and we now have constant access to the banqueting table of divine grace because of King Jesus. Because Jesus brought us to the table, our Father is *right there* to oversee and ensure we get all the nourishment we need. It's time to kick our scarcity mentality to the curb—we don't have to subsist on crumbs anymore because our Daddy owns the whole bakery, baby!

- **DO YOU EVER** tend to act like you are still an orphan in God's eyes? How so?

- **IN WHAT WAYS** do you sometimes subsist on "crumbs" in your Christian life?

- **HOW WOULD YOU** describe the relationship between approaching God with confidence and following God in obedience?

Day 22

AVOIDING A POWER OUTAGE

Jesus departed with his disciples to the sea, and a large crowd followed from Galilee, and a large crowd followed from Judea, Jerusalem, Idumea, beyond the Jordan, and around Tyre and Sidon. The large crowd came to him because they heard about everything he was doing. Then he told his disciples to have a small boat ready for him, so that the crowd wouldn't crush him. Since he had healed many, all who had diseases were pressing toward him to touch him. MARK 3:7–10

WHEN HE WAS ABOUT four or five years old, my little brother John got his first of many pet turtles, a little silver-dollar-sized one he named Myrtle. Unfortunately, Myrtle the Turtle was not long for this earth because a few mornings later, John came trudging up to the breakfast table with an expression of anguish and sadly announced that Myrtle was dead. Then he confessed he'd taken her out of her bowl the night before because he wanted to cuddle with her, but when he woke up, she wasn't moving anymore. Of course, Mom pretended his tiny turtle died from mysterious causes and got him another one right away. She didn't have the heart to tell him he'd accidentally smothered his first love to death. That's basically the scene here in Mark chapter 3; so many people are clamoring to get close to Jesus because of His reputation as a miraculous healer, He's in danger of being crushed!

It may sound innocuous, but one of the most potentially crushing demands of the Christian life is that *somebody will always need something from you.* Some people may even go so far as to demand for you to meet *all* their needs. But when we look at what the Bible teaches and demonstrates regarding human relationships, it's clear what God calls us to is interdependency, not codependency. That is, to make Him the main source we draw from and encourage others to as well since our Creator Redeemer is the only One with inexhaustible resources. He's the only One who has the capacity to be our emotional power grid! When we plug ourselves into anyone else or allow others to plug all of their emotional expectations into us, there's bound to be a lost connection or even a complete blackout. We'll end up smothered just like Myrtle, or, we might end up being the one who does the smothering!

However, when we learn to place the entirety of ourselves into God's perfect custody, we can freely enjoy rich life with others because our desire for unconditional love and acceptance is lying appropriately at His feet, not theirs. On one hand, when God is our power source, we can expect an appropriate amount of emotional energy from others without demanding that they fill us all the way up. And on the other hand, we can give an appropriate amount, knowing that our ministry matters to others, but that it's not all up to us to fill someone else's emotional cup to the brim. In both ways, whether giving or taking, we are free to *enjoy* others instead of *exploiting* others.

- **WHAT HUMAN INDIVIDUAL** do you place the majority of your emotional needs on? Do you think some of what you're expecting from them should actually come from Jesus?

- **WHO DO YOU** allow to smother you? How can you help this person see that the real way they are going to get filled up is through God—not you?

- **HOW MIGHT YOUR** relationships change if you believed God was the ultimate power source in your-and-their lives?

Day 23
GOING OUT WITH A BANG

Jesus let out a loud cry and breathed his last. Then the curtain of the temple was torn in two from top to bottom. When the centurion, who was standing opposite him, saw the way he breathed his last, he said, "Truly this man was the Son of God!" MARK 15:37–39

I'M NOT SURE WHAT was happening in the heart of God the Father when He heard that curtain rip, but the mama in me imagines that He was grinning from ear to ear! Remember, that drapery panel—which ancient rabbinic sources describe being as thick as a man's hand, weighing several thousand pounds and taking three hundred people to move—was torn completely in half. It's purpose? It separated the room called the "Holy of Holies" where the ark of the covenant was kept from the rest of the temple. Remember: "ark" is the Hebrew word for box, and so the "ark of the covenant" was—you guessed it—a box that held evidence of God's covenant with His people—holy relics like the stone tablets of the Ten Commandments.

Why did these things have to be separated, you ask? The Holy of Holies is where God's presence was. The rest of the temple is where everything else was. And only certain people at certain times under certain strict purification protocols could enter in the Holy of Holies without, you know, *dying.* You probably also remember that the ark of the covenant encompassed the "mercy seat" on which the high priest ceremonially sprinkled blood to atone for the sins of God's people during the high holy day of Yom Kippur (Exod. 25:18–21).

So when the veil was torn, the radical rip effectively removed the separation! Because Jesus paid the toll of death for sin, God's presence was now accessible! That's right, when that fancy fabric came crashing down it symbolically removed the separation between us and God's mercy! I also appreciate that Mark clarifies the curtain was torn from *top to bottom* (v. 38) implying that God's the One who initiated the rip.

And it was torn in two from top to bottom *at the ninth hour,* which means the divine "alteration" of that massive curtain—scholars approximate that it was sixty feet long and thirty feet wide—caused an *enormous* crash at three o'clock in the afternoon. Why does that matter? Because that was right about the time the temple priests were standing directly in front of it, dutifully going through the motions of religion. To say those poor guys had to be a *little* startled by all the commotion is like saying a bear is a *little* hungry when it wakes up from hibernation. One can't help but wonder if the revival that swept through the temple priesthood soon thereafter (Acts 6:7) was tied to this divinely inspired disturbance!

The curtain call (pun intended) of this whole Good Friday drama takes place when the centurion proclaimed the oh-so-obvious: *"Truly this man was the Son of God!"* At which point, I like to picture our heavenly Father laughing out load while saying to Himself, "You THINK?"

- **WHEN HAS THERE** been a figurative veil-tearing moment in your life when you felt like a barrier between you and God was removed?

- **WHEN DID YOU** first understand the core of the Gospel message—that Christ's work on the cross is what ripped down the barrier between you and God, giving you full access to the Father?

- **WHO IN YOUR** life might need to hear that God's presence is now available to them through Christ? Who do you see nearby in your life who still feels a "veil" between them and God, needing to hear that this veil has actually been torn down?

Day 24

GRACE GOGGLES

Let the whole earth shout triumphantly to the LORD!
Serve the LORD with gladness;
come before him with joyful songs.
Acknowledge that the LORD is God.
He made us, and we are his—
his people, the sheep of his pasture.
Enter his gates with thanksgiving
and his courts with praise.
Give thanks to him and bless his name.
For the LORD is good, and his faithful love endures forever;
his faithfulness, through all generations. PSALM 100

ONE OF MY FAVORITE writers (I actually have a pretty long "favorites" list because I love to read!), Frederick Buechner, wrote: "Listen to your life. See it for the fathomless mystery it is. In the boredom and pain of it, no less than in the excitement and gladness: touch, taste, smell your way to the holy and hidden heart of it, because in the last analysis all moments are key moments, and life itself is grace." And I found myself doing that very thing—listening to the miraculous heartbeat of my own life—while staying at Captiva Island in Florida recently with my Aunt Darlene, who's only eight years older than me and therefore more like a sister.

We were ambling along the shore at low tide in quiet companionship, both of us lost in our own thoughts, while Missy trailed behind us, happily examining shells and seaweed and the way periwinkle holes disappear then reappear with each wave. Darlene stopped in her tracks and asked sincerely, "Could you have imagined five years ago that you'd be visiting a place like this with your daughter?"

I thought about her question for a few seconds and then said, "No." I was going to say something else—being concise really isn't one of my strong suits— but I had to stop trying to speak because a giant lump of gratitude from my heart jumped into my throat and choked me into watery-eyed submission.

When God rescues you from a pit you dug yourself and carries you to an extraordinary, new chapter of life where His tangible redemption runs around in a bright blue swim cap and pink goggles squealing, "Look at this, Mama!" it's not hard to be overwhelmed with thanksgiving.

For you, redemption may not look just like mine did on that salty-aired day at the sea, but it looks like something. If you listen to your life, and really look to see where God's hand has been at work, miracles will surely show themselves.

- **WHEN YOU QUIET** the chatter in your head, and really listen to the miracle of your life, what are you most thankful for this season?

- **DO YOU CONSIDER** life itself a grace from God? Why or why not?

- **WHERE HAS GOD** carried you into a new chapter of life, showing you tangible redemption?

GET A GRIP

For I am persuaded that neither death nor life, nor angels nor rulers, nor things present nor things to come, nor powers, nor height nor depth, nor any other created thing will be able to separate us from the love of God that is in Christ Jesus our Lord. ROMANS 8:38–39

WHEN I WAS TWELVE or thirteen years old, my stepfather traded in his bass boat for a ski boat and decided to teach my sister, brother, and me how to slice across the surface of water on narrow boards at 30–40 miles an hour. One would think a feat like that would take a long time to master, but we learned to water ski pretty well in just one weekend because Dad Angel insisted that we learn in his favorite liquid hangout, the St. John's River. Which is a really gorgeous Floridian waterway, if you don't mind all the alligators!

Of course, he told us not to worry about all the floating "logs" that morphed into bumpy-backed monsters with big teeth, which we noticed with growing horror as we motored to the gator-infested stretch of river he decided was the perfect spot for beginner skiers. He went on to casually employ the same phrase I'll bet cavemen used to coax their kids outside when there was a T-Rex in their yard, too, "Now y'all don't worry. They're more afraid of you than you are of them." Yeah right. And real grizzlies are friendly toilet paper connoisseurs just like the cartoon ones in the Charmin commercials.

Needless to say, after Dad Angel gently shoved our floppy orange-vest-wearing selves over the side of the boat into the brackish brown water of the St. John's, we hung onto the ski rope as if our very lives depended on not letting go. Even after accidentally losing a ski when I careened across the wake, I refused to let go of the handle and gulped gallons of that nasty water while being dragged like a rag doll behind the boat. Because I knew if I did let go, there was a good chance I'd become gator kibble. And I've never been a big fan of being chewed on.

All of which brings me to an important spiritual point the pastor of Hebrews emphasized in triplicate to his congregation:

But Christ was faithful as a Son over his household. And we are that household if we *hold on* to our confidence and the hope in which we boast. (Heb. 3:6, emphasis mine)

For we have become participants in Christ if we *hold firmly* until the end the reality that we had at the start. (Heb. 3:14, emphasis mine)

Therefore, since we have a great high priest who has passed through the heavens—Jesus the Son of God—let us *hold fast* to our confession. (Heb. 4:14, emphasis mine)

Then he upped the ante in chapter 10 by adding the clause *without wavering:*

Let us *hold on* to the confession of our hope *without wavering,* since he who promised is faithful. (Heb. 10:23, emphasis mine)

In other words, don't just hold on, but hold onto to your faith in Jesus Christ and Don't. Let. Go. No. Matter. What. The really bad news of the Bible is that the devil is a dragon (Rev. 12), another aggressive carnivore with big teeth—basically the alligator's scriptural cousin. But the infinitely better news is that our hope isn't in the strength of our grip, it's in the supernaturally strong grasp of our God! Yes, we need to hold on to our faith for dear life, but never forget that God is holding on to us infinitely tighter! He's not letting go of us. Nothing can separate you from the love He has wrapped around you. So mimic Him, and hold on, friend!

- **WHAT OR WHO** has the power to make you loosen your grip on the Gospel?

- **HOW DOES KNOWING** there's an "enemy in the water" help you hold firmly to your faith?

- **HOW CAN YOU** remind yourself throughout the day that God is holding on to you?

Day 26

COSTLY COMMITMENT

When they heard this, everyone in the synagogue was enraged. They got up, drove him out of town, and brought him to the edge of the hill that their town was built on, intending to hurl him over the cliff. But he passed right through the crowd and went on his way. LUKE 4:28–30

THE ABOVE DRAMA IN Luke chapter 4 took place at a synagogue in Nazareth, where Jesus preached to a hometown crowd. During His message, He claimed to be the Messiah, the Son of God. And because they considered His claim to be heretical, the congregation was infuriated. Now you probably remembered that Nazareth was the hometown of Jesus, but what you may not know is that during this period of ancient history, Nazareth was a very small town with a population of only about 200–300 people. Which means lots of the folks who got mad at Jesus over the content of His sermon were His extended family members. It's one thing for your family to accuse you of being a nutjob. It's a whole other thing when your cousins conspire to hurl you off a cliff.

For some of you, your choice to follow Jesus has caused friction in your family. A few of you may even have been "disowned" by your parents or close relatives because your Christian faith is so contradictory to their belief system. I know—at least in part—how you feel. I will never forget the night when I was a senior in high school and my stepdad became so infuriated by my overt faith in Jesus Christ that he opened the front door and threw my beloved Bible out into the yard in the rain because he refused to have it in his house anymore. My Dad Harper had divorced Mom and left us when I was four years old; two years later Mom married John (whom I called Dad Angel), and by then I was pretty desperate for an adult male's affection and approval. It was devastating to be on the receiving end of my stepdad's agnostic anger.

By the absolute *grace* of God, Dad Angel put his faith in Jesus eight weeks before he died, a salvation that might have shocked the angels themselves! I can totally picture those heavenly emissaries glancing at each other with raised eyebrows when he strolled past on those streets of gold whispering, "Man, I didn't see that one coming!"

I'm incredibly grateful that my stepfather found peace with God two months before he died. However, the miraculous change at the very end of his life didn't magically give those of us who loved him *and* Jesus amnesia. Every now and then we still wince because of the deep emotional wounds he inflicted when he was so antagonistic toward our faith. The shrapnel caused by family members who oppose your relationship with God can cut you to the very bone. If you've experienced that kind of grief, I'm so sorry. I sincerely hope you find comfort in the fact that Mark's Gospel reveals our Savior knows exactly how we feel.

- **HAVE YOU EXPERIENCED** strain, pain, and/or stress in a relationship with someone you love as a result of your relationship with Jesus?

- **IF SO, ARE** you praying faithfully for them by name?

- **HOW DOES IT** encourage you that Jesus knows how you feel?

Day 27

WHEN YOUR SOCIOLOGY MATCHES YOUR THEOLOGY

"Then the righteous will answer him, 'Lord, when did we see you hungry and feed you, or thirsty and give you something to drink? When did we see you a stranger and take you in, or without clothes and clothe you? When did we see you sick, or in prison, and visit you?' "And the King will answer them, 'Truly I tell you, whatever you did for one of the least of these brothers and sisters of mine, you did for me.'" MATTHEW 25:37–40

ONE OF MY FAVORITE unsung heroes of the faith is Dr. Thomas Chalmers. He was born in 1780 in Scotland, in a small fishing community. He grew up in a pretty poor family, but one in which academics were highly valued. And before most children have mastered potty training, wee Master Chalmers' brilliance had bobbed to the surface. By the age of three he could read in English, Greek, and Hebrew. By the age of ten, he'd read every single book in the village where he lived with his mom, dad, and *thirteen* brothers and sisters! (Mrs. Chalmers, *you're a saint.*)

Long before he started shaving, young Tom was packed off to St. Andrews University. He finished his studies—getting advanced degrees in mathematics and theology—by the time he was nineteen. And by the time he was twenty, he was hired to be both a math professor at St. Andrews and the pastor of a small parish.

Of course, Chalmers' mental aptitude earned him the title of true genius. But the enormity of his cognitive IQ stood in stark contrast to his under-developed heart. Despite his intellect, he didn't "get" grace. He acted more like a jerk than like Jesus. He came across as arrogant and condescending and much more interested in ideas than individuals. Dr. George Grant, a pastor in Nashville and an expert on Chalmers, says during this stage of his life, "Chalmers was widely admired, but universally disliked!"

So, God gave Tom a providential time-out. After witnessing the premature deaths of two of his siblings from tuberculosis, he came down with the disease, too. He was bedridden for months and came very close to death. But it was in his weakened physical condition that he finally fell in love with His Savior.

He realized in his obsessive quest for knowledge about God, he'd forfeited an intimate relationship with God.

When he recovered his physical health, Chalmers resigned from his distinguished university position in order to pour himself into his rural community. He spent three days every week walking the countryside to visit people—whether they attended his church or not! His life became riddled with the language of love. By the time of his death in 1847, Thomas Chalmers had pioneered a vast and effective outreach to the poor and underprivileged; he helped build and pay for at least 500 new churches; initiated the construction and funding of more than 400 new schools; and had trained and deployed over 800 missionaries to foreign lands. Plus, he's one of the originators of the "soup kitchen" ministry method we still practice today, where the goal is to establish an urban center to feed and minister to the poor and homeless. Call it mercy ministry or social justice or compassionate activism or just plain old "living like Jesus"—what's clear is this: Dr. Chalmers was actually doing it long before it became a hashtag.

His compassionate sociology reflected his Christ-centered theology. He proved that if you really get God's grace for you, you'll slosh some measure of that same grace on the world around you. Which is sort of the whole point, isn't it?

- **IN YOUR EXPERIENCE,** what ways have you been the beneficiary of someone else's ministry?

- **HOW DOES THIS** experience teach and encourage you about the value of your own ministry?

- **WHAT/WHERE/WHO ARE SOME** of the dry places in your little corner of the world God has been prompting you to slosh grace on?

Day 28
TO EAT OR NOT TO EAT

"I continued fasting and praying before the God of heaven." NEHEMIAH 1:4 NET

— , · — — —

THE DEFINITION OF THE Greek word rendered "to fast" in the New Testament is: *abstaining from eating.* So, this practice of choosing to forgo food to increase our focus on God and faith in Him is an important part of Christian discipleship. After all, Jesus fasted forty days before He began His public ministry. But we need to be careful before we start putting down our forks and posting humble-brags on social media, because our Messiah actually warned about the potential dangers associated with fasting as often as He endorsed the activity.

For instance, when some men asked Jesus why His disciples didn't fast, our Savior equated fasting with sorrow and essentially said His homeboys wouldn't mourn until He left the proverbial building:

> Then they said to him, "John's disciples fast often and say prayers, and those of the Pharisees do the same, but yours eat and drink." Jesus said to them, "You can't make the wedding guests fast while the groom is with them, can you?" (Luke 5:33–34)

Then during the Sermon on the Mount, Jesus cautioned people about distorting the private discipline of fasting to get a public pat on the back:

> "Whenever you fast, don't be gloomy like the hypocrites. For they disfigure their faces so that their fasting is obvious to people. Truly I tell you, they have their reward. But when you fast, put oil on your head and wash your face, so that your fasting isn't obvious to others but to your Father who is in secret. And your Father who sees in secret will reward you." (Matt. 6:16–18)

Furthermore, long before Jesus advised His followers against fakey-fasting, God the Father reprimanded the Israelites about it:

"They act like a righteous nation that would never abandon the laws of its God. . . . 'We have fasted before you!' they say. 'Why aren't you impressed? We have been very hard on ourselves, and you don't even notice it!' 'I will tell you why!' I respond. 'It's because you are fasting to please yourselves. Even while you fast, you keep oppressing your workers. What good is fasting when you keep on fighting and quarreling? This kind of fasting will never get you anywhere with me.'" (Isa. 58:2–4 NLT)

Now before those of you in the Bible-banger-club—of which I'm a card-carrying member!—get your socks in a wad, of course there are *lots* of examples in Scripture where fasting is framed in a positive light, too! Like when the Jews obediently fasted to observe the Day of Atonement according to Old Testament law (Lev. 16:29); when Daniel fasted while repenting on behalf of God's people (Dan. 9:3–19); when Anna, an octogenarian female prophet, fasted while loitering around the temple hoping to meet the Messiah (Luke 2:36–38); when Jesus fasted for forty days while satan tempted Him in the desert (Matt. 4:1–11); and when faithful leaders in early church history fasted (Acts 10:30; 14:23). What do all those examples teach us? That fasting with a *pure heart* can be an effective way to humble ourselves and honor God during seasons of intense prayer and worship.

As Christ-followers, we must first rest in the fact that our Creator Redeemer *listens to us*—whether we're skipping meals or inhaling cheeseburgers—because *He loves us.* Then, after trusting God to be the perfect audience for all our prayers, it's a good idea to examine our motives for pushing away from the table. Are we choosing to fast to focus more intently on our heavenly Father, or to draw attention to our own devotion?

Only when the Holy Spirit gives us the green light to forgo food so as to draw near to God should we put down our forks. And if we don't get the go-ahead for a literal fast immediately, we can always practice "fasting" from criticism, self-absorption, and unkindness!

- **WHEN YOU'VE PRACTICED** self-denial in the past, do you think it was truly an expression of praise? Or was it an act—maybe even subconscious—of penance?

- **HOW HAVE YOU** seen God use fasting in your life for good?

- **WHAT MIGHT NEED** to change in your fasting habits to make them healthier or more biblical?

Day 29
THE BEST IS YET TO COME

For this world is not our permanent home; we are looking
forward to a home yet to come. HEBREWS 13:14 NLT

MY BIOLOGICAL DAD, WHO by now you know I sometimes call "Dad Harper," is named Everett Andrew Harper, and he was a Tootsie-roll pop kind of man. Hard on the outside, gooey on the inside. If you didn't really know him, his gruff voice, cowboy-like swagger, scuffed-up work boots, and the no-nonsense, synergistic way he was able to bark an order to someone on his construction crew—and spit tobacco juice with a sharp-shooter's precision at the same time—could be quite intimidating. (And I don't exaggerate when I say "cowboy-like." The man actually rode wild horses and bulls on the rodeo circuit to make extra money when he was in college, and always reminded my sister, Theresa, and me of a smaller version of John Wayne.)

As you can imagine, my high school and college boyfriends would get all wide-eyed and momentarily immobilized like a deer in the headlights of an automobile when they met him. But God dramatically softened my dad's heart in the last several decades of his life, transforming him into a caring father who called my sister and I multiple times a week and filled scores of prayer journals (which we discovered after he passed away) petitioning God on our behalf. He spent his latter years pouring into people less fortunate than himself. He became committed to hiring gentlemen who had difficulty getting jobs—like ex-cons and homeless men for his construction crew—and consistently swung wide the doors of his home to the occasional stray dog and recovering addict.

The cancer he nonchalantly knuckle-punched for over a decade finally killed him some years ago, and not a week goes by that I don't think about him and smile. One of the last things he whispered hoarsely to me a few days before he fell into a coma just prior to passing away was, "When is our baby girl comin' home?" He was referring to Missy because I was midway through the adoption process at that point. Despite his oh-so-stoic manner, deeply conservative roots, and the fact that I'd already been devastated by two failed adoption attempts, Dad was unreservedly supportive from the moment I told him God had prompted me to begin the risky process of adopting an HIV+ little girl from Haiti whose first mama had died from undiagnosed AIDS and whom doctors said didn't have much chance of survival herself.

And no matter how difficult our adoption journey got or how perilous Missy's health became, Dad remained resolute that our Creator Redeemer would make a way where there seemed to be no way and that Missy would become a "Harper girl" and his first granddaughter. I miss him terribly and grieve the fact that Missy didn't get to experience being fiercely loved by her granddaddy, but I also look forward to the day we're reunited in glory. I'm convinced we'll walk through those pearly gates to find Dad Harper standing there proudly next to some supernatural John Deere tractor with a smile on his face and detailed plans in his mind regarding how to teach his granddaughter to drive it.

- **HOW HAS EXPERIENCING** the death of a loved one affected the way you perceive heaven?

- **WHICH EMOTION DO** you experience more when you consider the idea of eternity—peace or uncertainty?

- **WHO HAS THE** Lord placed in your life to help you remember that God always makes a way—even through the hard stuff?

Day 30
TELL HIM WHERE IT HURTS

Then Job replied to the LORD:
I know that you can do anything
and no plan of yours can be thwarted.
You asked, "Who is this who conceals my counsel with ignorance?"
Surely I spoke about things I did not understand,
things too wondrous for me to know.
You said, "Listen now, and I will speak.
When I question you, you will inform me."
I had heard reports about you,
but now my eyes have seen you. JOB 42:1–5

———

SIR C. S. LEWIS (who I can't wait to meet in Glory since I've read every book he wrote at least twice and have nursed a platonic crush on him for decades) wrote: "Pain insists upon being attended to. God whispers to us in our pleasures, speaks in our consciences, but shouts in our pains. It is his megaphone to rouse a deaf world."[7] Which at first read might sound sober—if not depressing. However, over the past few years I've been surprised to discover that the deeper I'm willing to explore my own pain, the more joy I've been able to excavate.

We live in a world that is reeling in pain but doesn't know how to navigate it, so mankind goes to great lengths to numb it, to medicate their misery. Pharmacists are filling more anti-depression prescriptions than ever before in modern medical history, Internet porn sales are conservatively estimated to be *at least* 15 billion per year (yes, that's "b" for *billion*, putting it well ahead of Netflix in terms of profitability), and suicide in the United States increased by an alarming 30 percent from 2000–2016—50 percent among girls and women. To say the human race is not handling our pain well is a huge understatement.

And all too often contemporary culture flings blame in the wrong direction, much like a child snapping disrespectfully at a parent after school when what they're really upset about is the bully who knocked their plate over in the cafeteria at lunchtime. They're quick to ask angrily how a good God could allow horrific things like human trafficking and genocide and cancer to happen but very slow to acknowledge that *He is actually God*, whose ways are both superior to mankind's and above our comprehension and whose absolute sovereignty includes the ability to transform what is evil and tragic into something truly good.

Thankfully, as Christ-followers we have the antidote for global grief because like Job, we know there is a living, accessible, compassionate Redeemer who chooses to be close to the broken-hearted. When the world watches us express genuine peace and hope in the midst of suffering, the unlikeliness of our response captures their attention. As author Barbara Johnson used to say, "We are Easter People living in a Good Friday world!" In other words, how well we deal with heartbreak says everything about the One we've entrusted our hearts to. We're called to not simply be consumers of unlikely joy, but conduits to the world around us.

- **WHO IN YOUR** life exemplifies Barbara Johnson's description: "an Easter person living in a Good Friday world"?

- **DO YOU THINK** your close friends and family would describe you the same way?

- **WHAT MIGHT NEED** to shift in your life in order to develop this sort of unlikely perspective in the midst of pain?

Day 31
YOU CAN'T HIDE PRIDE

They came to Capernaum. When he was in the house, he asked them, "What were you arguing about on the way?" But they were silent, because on the way they had been arguing with one another about who was the greatest. MARK 9:33–34

"BUT THEY WERE SILENT." That phrase tickles me so much because I can totally picture that motley crew of *grown men* clamming up the way Missy sometimes does when she knows she's done something wrong and might face discipline for her bad choice. Which happened recently when she discovered how to use my Amazon account to download movies to her iPad (now in my sweet child's defense, this was in the first month of the COVID-19 pandemic when it was too cold to play outside and we were all feeling a bit stir-crazy up here on Missy's Mountain).

Me (when I walked upstairs to the TV room and found her sprawled out on the couch watching *Trolls World Tour* when she was supposed to be working on her math homework):

> Missy, why are you watching a movie instead of doing your homework? And wait a minute, isn't that the brand-new Trolls movie we saw on Amazon last night that cost $20 to download? Did you use my Amazon account to access this movie, Honey?

> Missy (looking directly at me with wide eyes and feigning innocence): *Hmmm?*

> Me (head now tilted a few degrees to one side and emphasizing each syllable of the question with a noticeably lower voice): *Did. You. Use. My. Amazon. Account. To. Download. This. Movie. Melissa?*

> Missy (now feigning interest in whatever was behind my head):

Crickets. Nada. Nothing. Suddenly the proverbial cat had shoplifted my normally chatty daughter's tongue and she had NO WORDS!

Honestly, I don't know why I even bothered to ask. Because unless we'd been invaded by aliens, Missy and I are the only folks with opposable thumbs who have access to my laptop during this quarantine season and unless somebody whacks me upside the head, I'm not inclined to pay twenty bucks for a movie about miniature blue people with super-annoying voices.

My smart little cookie of a daughter had gone and cracked my passcode to deceitfully download a new flick about her beloved Poppy and surely thought *UH OH!* when she heard me clomping up the stairs. It was all I could do to maintain my composure and not chuckle because watching her try to plead the fifth was actually pretty darn cute!

Don't you wish we could see the expression on Jesus' face as He watched His disciples become mute, feign innocence, and pretend to be interested in whatever was behind His holy head in this biblical scene? I can't wait to get to heaven and find out if my hunch is accurate because I'm convinced our Savior is a serial grinner! And His good nature is implied by the way He doesn't rebuke them for their childish behavior but instead gently scoops up a nearby toddler to use as a living metaphor in a patient attempt to get His followers to—as we would say here in the South—*act right!*

> He sat down, called the twelve disciples over to him, and said, "Whoever wants to be first must take last place and be the servant of everyone else." Then he put a little child among them. Taking the child in his arms, he said to them, "Anyone who welcomes a little child like this on my behalf welcomes me, and anyone who welcomes me welcomes not only me but also my Father who sent me." (Mark 9:35–37 NLT)

My guess is those burly men softened while watching their Lord and Savior affectionately cuddle a kid. Surely their defensive walls came tumbling down when He made eye contact with them while that peanut pulled on His beard, then winked before gently reminding them that it wasn't cool to elbow others out of the way in your quest to get to the front of the line.

- **WHO DO YOU** usually try to be "greater than" in your life? Why?

- **WHEN'S THE LAST** time you sensed God's Spirit gently chiding you for being too self-centered, or trying to get ahead of others for the spotlight?

- **DID YOU FEIGN** innocence initially? Or did you confess your culpability right away?

Day 32
HE GETS FIRST DIBS

When Jesus saw a large crowd around him, he gave the order to go to the other side of the sea. A scribe approached him and said, "Teacher, I will follow you wherever you go." Jesus told him, "Foxes have dens, and birds of the sky have nests, but the Son of Man has no place to lay his head." "Lord," another of his disciples said, "first let me go bury my father." But Jesus told him, "Follow me, and let the dead bury their own dead." MATTHEW 8:18–22

JESUS WASN'T SIMPLY A sojourner with no place to lay His head. He was abandoned and betrayed over and over and over again by those closest to Him. His mom and dad literally forgot Him at the temple when He was just a kid. His cousins tried to kill Him. His best friend threw Him under the bus at His greatest point of need, just prior to His murder on the cross. Surely our Savior's Enneagram number was 13 because of the unlucky hand He was dealt relationally!

As we know, Jesus kept at it, even when His community gave up on Him. And please don't hear me wrong—I'm not trying to imply that human relationships aren't necessary or significant. Quite the contrary, I believe community is critical. Just think of the apostle John's encouragement to love other people well because that's how the world will know we're followers of Christ (John 13:34–45). Then there's Lesslie Newbigin, who made one of my all-time favorite observations about community: "I am suggesting that the only answer, the only hermeneutic of the Gospel, is a congregation of men and women who believe it and live by it."[8] In other words, we actually see Jesus most clearly when we view Him through the lens of other people!

Trust me, I'm an ardent fan of authentic friendships. Several times while we were quarantined during COVID-19, I drove over to dear friends' homes and stood in their yards so I could at least see them through their window while we chatted instead of over a computer screen! Doing life with other people is a divine gift . . . community is significant and life-giving and sacred.

However, even in the life of Christ, it's obvious that our horizontal relationships with other humans *must* be subordinate to our relationship with God. Whether our relationships are giving us all sorts of life and encouragement, or they are trying to throw us under the bus, the truth is this: He comes first, period.

- **HOW CAN YOU** see the value of community in Jesus' life, but also the dedication to the Father as primary to Him?

- **WHAT HUMAN RELATIONSHIPS** get the bulk of your attention and affection?

- **WHAT ARE YOU** intentionally doing to ensure they stay in second place, behind God?

Day 33
REDEMPTIVELY ROPED IN

Two are better than one because they have a good reward for their efforts. For if either falls, his companion can lift him up; but pity the one who falls without another to lift him up. Also, if two lie down together, they can keep warm; but how can one person alone keep warm? And if someone overpowers one person, two can resist him. A cord of three strands is not easily broken. ECCLESIASTES 4:9–12

———————

I CAN'T SHAKE THIS conviction that's been loitering in my soul for a while now: far too many of my friends, and friends of friends have lost their joy and all but lost their faith in Jesus. Many have shared with me how they've completely stopped going to church or Bible study or even hanging out with other believers. Usually because the deepest wound they're nursing was inflicted by a professing Christian or religious institution. Or because they've simply lost the energy and will to put on a happy face and pretend, which has been the sum total of their previous experience in communities of faith.

Surely our God weeps over the gaping holes in the fabric of His covenant family. We weren't created to be wincing, jaded isolationists. There's no such thing as successful Lone-Ranger-Christian living. We were created in God's image, in the image of the only Triune Creator-Redeemer who exists in perfect relational harmony with Himself as Father, Son, and Spirit ("Let *us* make man in *our* image" Gen. 1:26, emphasis mine). Which essentially means, we're hardwired for relationship—for the sacrament of communing with others.

If you're in a disillusioned, despairing kind of lonely season, I strongly encourage you not to limp into a corner with your back to the bride of Christ. Instead find a motley crew of passionate—albeit flawed—Christ-followers to assist you as you hobble toward healing. Find two or three sweet-spirited saints who will commit to pray with you and for you on a regular face-to-face basis. Take comfort in the fact that you can hurl all the sad, angry, and disappointed words you've been saving up toward the heavens because God is perfectly safe to share them with.

And finally, recruit someone who's walked closely with Jesus longer than you have to help tutor you in the subject of keeping in step with the Holy Spirit.

Someone who will be both wildly and graciously *for you* as well as completely and redemptively honest *with you*. Someone who'll actually speak up when you cross the line from legitimate grief-bearing to illegitimate victimhood-mentality. Lean in even when it's hard, lest you lose what's actually worth living for.

- **WHO ARE THE** other spiritual musketeers you trust enough to ride alongside this season?

- **WHAT USUALLY TRIGGERS** you to pull away from community?

- **HOW CAN YOU** anticipate this trigger and fight it well?

Day 34

LAZY FAITH = SPIRITUAL DROWNING

For this reason, we must pay attention all the more to what we
have heard, so that we will not drift away. HEBREWS 2:1

FROM YOURS TRULY, HERE is some fun Bible trivia you can use, free of charge, to dazzle your friends at the next church potluck. "Drift away" in this verse comes from the Greek word *pararreo*—line over the "o" giving it a hard "oh" sound. (If your initial thought was, "Oh, kind of like Camero?" you are not alone). This word basically means "slip away" or "flow past," which comes off a bit innocuous initially, right? Like some teenager sprawled out on an inner tube, floating down a lazy river in a Mountain Dew commercial. However, as I learned one summer a few years ago, floating can actually be much more dangerous than it looks.

I was at the beach, almost asleep in a lounge chair, when I noticed a woman flailing in the surf about fifty or so yards out in the sea. There weren't any lifeguards on this particular stretch of sand in Northern Florida, so I looked around to see if anyone else was watching, but there were only a handful of other sunbathers around and nobody was paying attention to the screaming chick. So I instinctively jumped up and ran into the waves to retrieve her.

I spent six summers working as a lifeguard in high school and college, and my old training kicked in as I approached her. I spoke calmly and assured her she was going to be okay when I got close enough for her to hear me, then I made a shallow dive underwater, grabbed her by the thighs and turned her body so that I could put her in a cross-chest carry. One of the first things you learn in lifeguard training is never to approach a panicked swimmer directly because their instinct is to grab whoever's closest around the neck, which is why there are so many double-drowning incidents.

Anyway, after I got her in a floating position on her back with my right arm over her chest, I began stroking with my left arm and scissor-kicking as hard as I could with both legs toward shore. But within a few moments alarm bells began going off in my head because instead of making any forward progress we were quickly getting pulled further and further out to sea.

I asked her to help me kick so that we could make some headway but all she did was mumble incoherently, which is when I smelled the alcohol and realized she reeked of beer. I was probably in the water with that woman for another four or five minutes when it occurred to me that we might not make it. The surf was just so rough, she was such dead weight, and I'd inhaled so much seawater that I started seeing white stars—the way you do just before you faint. It's the only time in my entire life that I was actually afraid I was going to drown.

I believe it was only the grace of God that gave me the strength to finally drag Ms. Bud Light to the shore where we both collapsed face down in the sand like Tom Hanks in *Castaway*. By then I was so beat, I decided to head back to the hotel as soon as I was able to hand her off to the party of drunks she'd wandered off from. When the manager saw me walking into the lobby, he asked why I was coming in earlier than usual. After I explained why I was so physically and mentally spent he exclaimed, "Oh Lisa, you're lucky to be alive because the riptide was so strong today, the Weather Service warned people not to get in the water at all!" He went on to describe soberly how two tourists had already drowned that day only a mile or so up the coast from us. And that's when I realized why it had been more difficult than usual to swim boozer-babe to safety. The whole time I was trying to move us toward the beach, there was a powerful current—lethally powerful—pulling us in the other direction.

Which is basically the same condition we find ourselves in as followers of Christ. Treading water spiritually is not a viable option. Because if we aren't intentionally moving toward Jesus, there is a powerful riptide of an enemy *actively working* to pull us away from Him. There's no such thing as neutral waters. "Don't Drift" isn't an innocuous biblical warning, it's a flashing red light accompanied by a blaring siren!

- **WHAT'S THE ONE** thing that most tempts you to drift in your pursuit of the Lord?

- **WHAT ARE YOU** intentionally doing to keep yourself moving toward Jesus instead of drifting away from Him?

- **IF YOU ARE** in a season of spiritual drift, who is a solid believer nearby that God may have placed in your life to help you paddle back to shore?

Day 35
THE APPLE OF GOD'S EYE

"As the Father has loved me, I have also loved you. Remain in my love." JOHN 15:9

ONE OF MY FAVORITE living authors is a lovely, humble pastor named Max Lucado. I've had the joy of getting to know Max, his wife Denalyn, and their three daughters a bit over the past twenty years, but prior to the undeserved privilege of meeting them personally, a friend shared something she observed about Max while at a party in their home that I will never forget. He was deep in conversation with several publishing executives and industry leaders when their daughter Jenna—who was probably six or seven at the time—began to play a song she'd just learned on the piano to entertain a few guests in the adjacent room. My friend said Max graciously excused himself from conversing with those notable executives, walked over to the room where his little girl was playing that basic tune, leaned against the wall and watched her with a big, proud smile stretched across his face. Surely her father's simple, yet intentionally preferential gesture made Jenna feel like the most important person in the room.

Henri Nouwen is another one of my favorite authors, and in his classic book *The Wounded Healer* he makes an exquisitely poignant observation that reminds me of that precious moment Max shared with his daughter:

> Everyone who returns from a long and difficult journey is looking for someone waiting for him at the station or airport. Everyone wants to tell his story and share his moments of pain and exhilaration with someone who stayed home, waiting for him to come back.[9]

In other words, we all *ache* for someone who loves us enough to listen to our whole story regardless of how demanding the rest of their day was. Someone who will wait for us to return home, regardless of where we journeyed off to. Someone who will always make us feel like the most important person in the room, regardless of who else is there. Fortunately, the Bible makes it clear that's *exactly* who Jesus is . . . the King of all kings is also the One leaning against a wall, gazing at us with tender affection while we play "Chopsticks."

- **DO YOU FEEL** confident enough in God's love for you to keep playing your version of "Chopsticks" if you could see Him watching you? Or do you think you'd freeze up with insecurity and cower in fear?

- **DO YOU OFTEN** forget God's smiling demeanor toward you? Why?

- **WHAT'S ONE GOD-GIVEN** hobby or interest you have that, if you pursued it a little more, could bring God great delight?

Day 36
BODY BUILDING

And let us consider one another in order to provoke love and good works, not neglecting to gather together, as some are in the habit of doing, but encouraging each other, and all the more as you see the day approaching. HEBREWS 10:24–25

OFTENTIMES I'M NOT ABLE to get a flight home until the morning after a conference, and for whatever reason, being trapped in unfamiliar places causes me to crave Indian food. Because there's nothing quite like copious amounts of warm naan and Chicken Tikka Masala to restore exhausted, spicy-food loving Bible teachers! Anyway, not too long ago, I found myself in a far-from-home city with an airport that rolled up its sidewalks at sundown, so I Googled "Indian food" and soon found myself shoveling forkfuls of basmati rice and curry-covered chicken into my mouth. I may've moaned in ecstasy at one point.

After consuming enough food to feed a football lineman, I booked an Uber to take me back to the hotel. I tried to act graceful and nonchalant when the driver pulled up, but I'm pretty sure the way I waddled to his car with beads of sweat on my upper lip from my super-spicy supper gave my gluttony away. In an effort to distract him from the fact that I had to unbutton the top of my jeans (or else ask him to swing by a hospital because I'd cut off my circulation), I casually asked him how his night was going. Of course, I didn't have a lot of emotional investment into his well-being at that point. All I really wanted to do was get back to my room at the Marriott as quickly as possible so that I could be miserable in private. I was surprised when instead of responding with the usual and non-committal, "fine," he turned around to face me and replied sincerely, "I'm not doing too well tonight, Ma'am, but I'm sure you don't feel like hearing my sad story on a Saturday night." And just like that, a spark of compassion elbowed my indigestion out of the way.

I said, "My name's Lisa and I'd love to hear your story." Which was all it took to open the door to Jason's heart. He explained that his wife had been murdered in a fast-food-robbery gone bad a few years before, and that he was raising their three young children by himself. He teared up while talking about how much he missed his wife and how he wished she could be there to see their youngest daughter start kindergarten the following week. His raw authenticity gave me the perfect opportunity to talk about God's tangible comfort during life's most painful seasons. How the Bible promises that He's close to the brokenhearted and near to us when our lives feel crushed (Ps. 34:18).

At that point Jason's countenance lit up and he began sharing enthusiastically about how God had been the foundation of their healing process from the very beginning. A smile spread across his face when he described how their oldest son—who was nine at the time—walked into his bedroom the morning after his mama was killed and said, "Daddy, I think we need to start going to church." The last five minutes of our ride became a rolling revival as we swapped stories about how loving and accessible God is. Instead of simply being a mode of transportation, his vehicle morphed into a sanctuary!

Though it was unexpected, our God-authored connection reminded me of how important it is for believers to share the cool stuff Christ is doing in our lives and encourage each other by testifying what our Redeemer *has actually redeemed* in our little corner of the world! Frankly, I think it's an absolute necessity for those of us who are committed to staying the course of radical Christian living. Because if you don't want to veer off the trail and get all banged up and bloodied on the rocks of self-pity and discouragement, you need Christian community. Isolation (as well as the kind of groan-inducing indigestion that follows the overconsumption of curry) came with the Fall. But with Christ and others by our side, we don't have to let the Fall call the shots anymore. We can invite others in and share in God's victory together. If we'd only be brave enough to talk about it.

- **WHEN'S THE LAST** time you shared something encouraging that God has done in your life with someone whose shoulders seemed to be sagging?

- **HOW HAS SOMEONE** else's story of God's work in their life increased your faith?

- **WHY DO YOU** think you sometimes shy away from sharing what Christ is doing in your square inch of the world?

Day 37
LETTING GO FOR GOOD

"For God loved the world in this way: He gave his one and only Son, so that everyone who believes in him will not perish but have eternal life. For God did not send his Son into the world to condemn the world, but to save the world through him." JOHN 3:16–17

————————

I'VE GOTTEN A LOT of parenting credit I don't deserve over the fact that Missy and I had an uncommonly smooth adoption transition. And while I'd like to think she connected with me so quickly because I'm such a good mama, the truth is our relatively fast and deep mother-daughter bond is Fifi's fruit. Fifi is Missy's great-aunt. She's the sickly, gentle, huge-hearted saint who took my little girl in when her lovely biological mama was too sick from AIDS (which she never knew she had because, like far too many impoverished people barely surviving in Third World countries, Marie had never been diagnosed) to care for her. Marie was simply too weak to produce milk, much less scrounge for food for her infant. Too cold to snuggle her daughter at night and provide necessary warmth. So Fifi stepped in to rescue Missy and is the main reason my baby girl survived infancy. Fifi is also the one who championed me to be her new mama, because though she had stepped in to care for Missy soon after she was born, she's elderly and suffers with serious health problems herself, so she didn't have the capacity to do so long term. Missy needed a forever mama, and Fifi helped make that happen. In spite of the fact that I was an American stranger who, if approved to adopt her beloved great-niece, would take her to a land far, far away filled with four-wheel drive trucks and fried food called Tennessee.

The first time I met Fifi she smiled shyly and then placed this scowling toddler named Missy into my arms and said to her firmly in Creole, "This is your white mama." Both Missy and I protested; I wanted to give Missy ample time to warm up to me and Missy was obviously alarmed by my pale ampleness. But Fifi just smiled again shyly, crossed her arms, and quietly refused to take the indignant two-and-a-half-year-old back into her embrace. It took a few minutes for Missy to quit trying to wriggle out of my arms but when she realized she didn't have a choice in the matter, she grudgingly relented to let me feed her beans and rice.

The next day, at Fifi's insistence, Missy allowed me to hold her hand and walk around the village for an hour. The second night I was there, Missy condescended to sit on my lap during a stifling hot worship service, after Fifi gave her a very direct you'd-better-mind-me-right-now-young-lady look. With each new baby-step milestone in our budding relationship, Fifi's smile got wider and she'd nod with approval. When I hugged her fiercely before leaving at the end of that first of many visits, all the while babbling about how grateful I was, she replied simply, "I love you, praise Jesus"—one of the only English phrases she knew.

Over the next two years those five words became our regular conversation. During long, hot, bumpy bus rides together from their village to Port-au-Prince for a doctor's checkup or an appointment with the US Embassy, Fifi would hold my hand the entire two- to three-hour trip and repeat softly, "I love you, praise Jesus" every so often. When I tried to engage her with my pitiable attempts to speak Creole (I still have several introduction to Creole books in my library and an "easy" English-Creole app on my phone but much like Frenchy in the musical *Grease*, I proved to be a language school drop-out), she'd nod and listen patiently but would inevitably respond with, "I love you, praise Jesus."

Finally, on April 14, 2014, when I hugged Fifi with tears streaming down my face, Missy sleeping in my arms, and clutching a manila folder with Haitian and American documents stating that I was now legally Missy's adoptive mother, she squeezed both of my hands, looked deep into my eyes and said again, "I love you, praise Jesus." By then I knew what she really meant by those five words was, "I'm entrusting you to take good care of her. It's breaking my heart to know I'll probably only see her again a few more times before I die, but I know this is what's best for her. Remember that she likes her mangos on the firm side and she loves to be sung to sleep. Don't let her be lazy in school, or be disrespectful, or eat with her mouth open, or bite her fingernails or forget how very much I love her. Okay, I'm going to kiss her head one last time and try to memorize her face and her precious little girl smell and the shape of her toes before I turn my head. And please know the reason I won't watch you drive away toward the airport isn't because I'm ambivalent . . . it's so I won't chase the van and beg you not to leave quite yet."

Fifi willingly gave up her claim on my daughter's heart so that my daughter could live. Hers is one of the most sacrificial affections I've ever had the privilege of witnessing. How much more so is our heavenly Father's affection for us?

The situations are obviously different between Missy and Jesus, I know. But after experiencing that day with Fifi, I can't help but be amazed that God willingly watched His only begotten Son depart from Glory knowing that He would be pierced for our transgressions. With the full knowledge that Jesus would soon scream in agony, "Dad, *Dad*, why have You forsaken Me?" God also knew He would have to choose not to lift a finger to help His incarnate child when He cried out from that cursed tree. Because in order for His image-bearers to live, His boy had to die. That God would part ways—even momentarily—with His own child. For you. For me. For all of us. What sacrifice!

- **HAS GOD EVER** prompted you to sacrificially step back from a relationship with someone you love for their own good? Maybe with one of your children as they prepare to leave home and become more independent?

- **IF SO, HOW** did you respond?

- **WHERE MIGHT GOD** be calling you to give up something precious to you for the greater good?

Day 38
RED-FACED AND RED-HANDED

For I know that nothing good lives in me, that is, in my flesh. For the desire to do what is good is with me, but there is no ability to do it. ROMANS 7:18

———

A FEW WEEKS AGO I was driving down a country road near our house, humming a worship chorus off-key, while Missy sang along in perfect pitch, sounding every bit as good as the voice on the radio (not that I'm biased or anything) from the backseat. Suddenly I thought, *Hmmmm, I never noticed that weird sound in this song before?* because just then I began to hear a kind of high-pitched keening over the sound of my daughter's melodic voice. It took me a few seconds to realize it was a state trooper with his blue lights flashing behind me! I'm not normally a fast driver, so I rarely get pulled over, but when I do, I get flustered. I think my anxiety stems from watching a *Charlie's Angels* episode when I was in middle school about a crooked sheriff who planted drugs in Farrah's trunk after pulling her over.

Anyway, when the officer walked up to my window, lowered his sunglasses, and asked in a slow, disapproving drawl, "Do you have any idea what you were doing back there, ma'am?", I blurted out nervously, "No, sir, but I'm sure it was bad!" Long story short, he ended up being very nice and graciously let me off with a warning since I wasn't going that much over the speed limit. But my shrill confession—*I'm sure it was bad!*—had me rolling my eyes at myself for the rest of the day!

I bear a striking resemblance to Paul's self-portrait: *What I don't understand about myself is that I decide one way, but then I act another, doing things I absolutely despise* (Rom. 7:15 The Message*).* So for me repentance isn't just the singular act of confessing that I did something ungodly and need my heavenly Father's forgiveness for that specific sin; it's the *continual awareness* that I will always do ungodly things without His guidance and correction and the transformative power of the Holy Spirit. It's my uninterrupted plea for sanctification. It's my moment-by-moment spiritual *mea culpa.* It's the life-rope I've attached to God's holiness so I won't drift away from the awesome destiny He's designed especially for me. It's the position of humility that keeps me happily secure under His protective wings. It's the daily, proverbial Post-It note reminding me that only God is the sovereign ruler of the universe and He doesn't need my input. It's my road to personal revival, as well as I believe the only route to corporate revival (2 Chron. 7:14). And for me, repentance doesn't always express itself in head-bowed, red-faced penance before Jesus either. In fact, more often than not it's expressed with a head-bobbing, happy dance because I'm so overjoyed by the intimacy repentance affords me with the King of all kings!

- **HOW WOULD YOU** describe the feeling of divine forgiveness that has followed your repentance?

- **DO YOU REPENT** often in your daily walk with God? Why or why not?

- **WHAT HOLDS YOU** back from using the gift of repentance that God has granted us all?

Day 39

A FAITH WORTH FIGHTING FOR

I solemnly charge you before God and Christ Jesus, who is going to judge the living and the dead, and because of his appearing and his kingdom: Preach the word; be ready in season and out of season; correct, rebuke, and encourage with great patience and teaching. For the time will come when people will not tolerate sound doctrine, but according to their own desires, will multiply teachers for themselves because they have an itch to hear what they want to hear. They will turn away from hearing the truth and will turn aside to myths. But as for you, exercise self-control in everything, endure hardship, do the work of an evangelist, fulfill your ministry. For I am already being poured out as a drink offering, and the time for my departure is close. I have fought the good fight, I have finished the race, I have kept the faith. 2 TIMOTHY 4:1–7

RECENTLY, AFTER PULLING SEVERAL all-nighters, I finished a seminary paper I had been working on for some time. After that paper was turned in, I got to hit a new milestone—being three-quarters of the way through the classroom portion of my doctoral studies. Which means only two and a half more years to go before graduation! Quite a few concerned friends have asked why in the world I chose to go back to school in my mid-fifties since I already have a very full life. When one asked how long exactly it will take to finish my doctorate, I explained that if I stay on pace with the required classes, research methodology, and thesis development, I hope to graduate the summer I turn sixty. As you can imagine, she burst out laughing and proclaimed, "Lisa, you ain't right!" When it comes to this sentiment, you might be surprised to find that I whole-heartedly agree! The way I see it, I've always been a bit of an outlier! (Well, as much as a theologically conservative white woman who grew up in the southeastern United States and is often clad in stretchy pants can be anyway.)

Plus, I believe this later-in-life, uphill academic quest to help prove the Bible is a love story from cover to cover—that God has always been and will always be *for us*—is totally worth the effort. Why? Because I've noticed an increasing shift among Christian women away from biblically faithful churches and culture. The consistent rationale is their negative experience with pastors and spiritual leaders who manipulate Scripture to propagate and/or justify the marginaliza-tion of other image-bearers. And that has flat broken my heart because I think without the grace and guidance of God's Word, the intimate connection we were created to enjoy with Him is hugely limited. I also believe biblical revelation is one of the primary ways for all human beings (regardless of gender, ethnicity, or cultural background) to understand—in part—the historical transcendence of God, which is a key element in understanding our worth and purpose in this world. The bottom line is: if we toss out the perfectly holy and holistically redemptive theme of Scripture because some people were jerks in the way they handled complex passages, we will be so stinkin' confused about our inherent value and the miraculous accessibility we have to our Creator-Redeemer.

If you can't tell by now, those are the things I'm passionate about, and I don't want to stop learning about them and inviting other people in to see their worth. Therefore, I'm thrilled I get to pull all-nighters studying instead of daydreaming about retirement at this age and stage of my life! Frankly, I think my heart would get bored silly if "coasting for Jesus" was my life strategy. I don't want to coast. I want to keep climbing. Up into my calling. Up into more knowledge and experience of God. Up into the things that matter. Don't you?

It may not look like registering for doctoral studies, but I'm sure you have things you're super-passionate about, too. Things God has called you into. Things He built you to do all the way to the end of your race. Don't start slowing down now, friend. Onward, upward, and outward!

- **HOW HAVE YOU** been "poured out" for Jesus and others lately?

- **WHAT UPHILL RACES** of faith are you still excited about running?

- **WHERE HAVE YOU** been coasting in your faith, and how can you start climbing again?

Day 40
PERFECTLY HITCHED

"Listen to me, Jacob,
and Israel, the one called by me:
I am he; I am the first,
I am also the last.
My own hand founded the earth,
and my right hand spread out the heavens;
when I summoned them,
they stood up together.
This is what the LORD, your Redeemer, the Holy One of Israel says:
I am the LORD your God,
who teaches you for your benefit,
who leads you in the way you should go."
ISAIAH 48:12–13, 17, EMPHASIS MINE

FOR REASONS THAT NOW seem less compelling in retrospect, I decided to rent an RV travel trailer and take Missy and my nephew John Michael camping for Fall break this year. Since we all enjoy hiking and biking in the great outdoors, I guess I thought toting a tin shelter behind our very own vehicle would be a great way to immerse ourselves more fully into our adventures. That staying on-site in a remote, wilderness area with a well-earned reputation for black bear activity would be really enjoyable and *relaxing.*

Of course, once I made that bold decision, I spent more time ordering cute camping paraphernalia—like matching outdoor chairs and darling headlamps and new hiking outfits—from Amazon than I did considering how difficult pulling a two-ton, twenty-one foot RV behind our mid-size SUV on the Interstate during a thunderstorm and high winds was going to be. Nor did I practice making the exaggeratedly wide turns one must master in order to pull such an unwieldy contraption into gas stations without coming perilously close (4 inches to be exact) to crashing into the low cement wall protecting the gasoline tanks. (In my defense, another RV was hogging the bulk of the pull-through lane.)

By the time we got to Big South Fork National Park—3 hours from our house by car, 5 hours when hauling a heavy RV with a rebellious spirit—my hands were cramping from white-knuckling the steering wheel and my nerves felt like they'd been tasered several times. And just when I thought our misadventure couldn't get any more zany/wacky/emotionally debilitating, we discovered that the camping spot we'd reserved a month earlier—now the only camping spot with RV hookups left for miles and miles around in light of it being peak season for fall leaf peeping—was one that required *backing up into from the bottom of a steep hill on a very narrow, single road with steep drop-offs on either side!*

How in the world I managed to get that huge thing parked without taking out a big tree (saplings don't count)—or John Michael who bravely stood in my blind spot and attempted to give me directions—is still a mystery to me. But I can tell you I swaggered a bit while walking to the bathhouse later that evening. That is, after I jumped completely off the ground (a feat I didn't know I was still capable of) and shrieked loud enough to alert a park ranger because I'm pretty sure I saw a snake in the bushes between our crookedly parked trailer and the communal potties.

But all in all, two nights of complete insomnia (alas, my creaky, middle-aged bones aren't used to slumbering on an egg-crate "mattress," much less in our teeny, weeny coffin-like "sleeping alcove"), copious bug bites, and all of the anxiously choreographed midnight and pre-dawn hops to the bathhouse (my bladder seems to be shrinking at the same rate my hair is graying) were totally worth it. *Why*, you may ask? Because three days after all the somewhat traumatizing fun began—after we hitched everything back up and after John Michael had chivalrously dumped the "black water" (yes, I told him I'd gladly pay for his therapy)—and we started the long journey home, Missy—who seemed to love every, single moment of our misadventure—sighed happily and proclaimed, "Mom, you're my BFF!" *Mother and best friend . . .* two titles I don't deserve but will definitely spend the rest of my life gratefully devoted to being. Even if it means renting a bigger RV next fall.

You've probably noticed by now that I often use two titles to refer to God as well: *Creator* and *Redeemer.* Although the Bible technically only couples them together once (in the title of Isaiah 48 rsv), they are as firmly hitched in my heart and mind as our SUV and that rolling metal house/bane of my recent existence. Because Creation marks the beginning of human history, which quickly leads—much like a supernatural domino effect—to mankind's desperate need for redemption. Making "Creator" and "Redeemer" hand-in-glove is miraculous in my estimation, because it shows off the twin facets of a fantastically faithful God, who loves us too much to leave us in the pit we dug ourselves. Or jack-knifed backward up a big hill, as it were.

- **HOW WOULD YOU** explain the connection between God's titles of Creator and Redeemer?

- **HOW DOES IT** encourage you that God didn't just create the world and then leave it to its own devices after the fall?

- **WHAT OTHER TITLES** of God are your favorites? Why?

Day 41

THE UNDERRATED BEAUTY OF A BASEMENT

"Blessed are you who are hungry now, because you will be filled. Blessed are you who weep now, because you will laugh." LUKE 6:21

———————

SOME YEARS AGO I lost two people who mattered very, very much to me. I was also diagnosed with cancer during that same time frame, which made for a sad fall season. I felt like my feet had been knocked right out from under me. By God's grace the cancer ended up being a "non-invasive, no big deal" situation because a surgeon was able to excise it with outpatient surgery. But the death of my stepdad coupled with the death of another long-term relationship were the straws that broke my emotional camel's back.

I'd always been a pull-myself-up-by-the-bootstraps kind of person, but I lost my ability to be self-sufficient on the heels of those losses. Over the next few weeks—as I was desperately trying to dig myself out of the deep, dark hole I found myself in—I kept hearing the Lord tenderly whisper to my battered heart, "Lisa, you've been running scared from sorrow for far too long. So I'm going to take you down to the basement of your life and sit there with you in the dark until that fear doesn't own you anymore."

Little did I know the beautiful, redemptive, joy-saturated, season that I'm standing in now would begin in an emotional basement. Because during those pitch-black nights of the soul I realized that my old habit of not entrusting God with my grief had also greatly hindered my capacity to access His compassion. I finally learned that one of the most valuable gifts we can give the world around us—a culture that's obviously wrestling in the dark with deep pain—is to quit pretending like we've never ached, and instead authentically testify to God's ability to heal us. To meet us in the dark and to help us find our way forward.

I've often heard my dear friend Christine Caine use an illustration about how the most flavorful oils and wines are produced through a crushing process to emphasize the value of hardship in our lives when it's sifted through the hands of God. And I'm convinced that if I hadn't been through my own crushing season, I never would've experienced the oil of gladness that came with the much deeper bonds I have with friends and family now, nor the indescribable joy of getting to be Missy's second mama. Trusting God with my hurt stretched my heart in such a way that it could carry a lot more love. In my experience, the loveliest blooms grow in soil that has been softened by tears.

- **WHAT BLOOMS HAVE** you noticed in the tear-soaked seasons of your life? Do you think anyone else noticed them?

- **DO YOU NEED** to go with God to your emotional basement in this season? Why might you be afraid to follow Him there?

- **DO YOU BELIEVE** God is powerful enough to meet you in the dark, and help you find your way forward? How have you seen Him do this already in your past?

Day 42

THE DISCORDANT TUNE OF TOOTING YOUR OWN HORN

James and John, the sons of Zebedee, approached him and said, "Teacher, we want you to do whatever we ask you." "What do you want me to do for you?" he asked them. They answered him, "Allow us to sit at your right and at your left in your glory." Jesus said to them, "You don't know what you're asking. Are you able to drink the cup I drink or to be baptized with the baptism I am baptized with?" "We are able," they told him. Jesus said to them, "You will drink the cup I drink, and you will be baptized with the baptism I am baptized with. But to sit at my right or left is not mine to give; instead, it is for those for whom it has been prepared." When the ten disciples heard this, they began to be indignant with James and John. MARK 10:35–41

THE MOTLEY CREW OF twelve disciples is now several years into an itinerant world mission project led by Jesus. They've heard Him teach multiple times about meekness, servanthood, and how the last will be first. The Son of God has also soberly informed them three times by now (Mark 8:31–32; 9:31; 10:32–34) that He's going to be murdered right around the corner in Jerusalem. Yet they're still so infected with a "What's in it for me?" mentality, they can't stop fussing about who gets to ride shotgun.

Their presumptuous request probably relates back to His promise that the disciples would sit on twelve thrones with Him in heaven (Matt. 19:28). But these two prideful siblings foolishly laid an earthly template over His divine promise and were jockeying for the best position *in Glory!* My goodness, that'd be like if a troll who lived under a bridge was graciously invited into a philanthropist's mansion for dinner but instead of displaying gratitude, he plopped his grimy self down on a spotless, antique dining chair and demanded fresh-caught lobster as his first course.

The world says, *Push to the front of the line!* Jesus says, *Go to the back of the line.*

The world says, *Brand yourself and blast your accomplishments all over social media!* Jesus says, *If you want to be great you have to first learn to serve.*

The King of all kings laid down His scepter in Glory and condescended to become man. Not a man from an impressive lineage, background, or position either. He chose to be born in a barn to an unwed teen-aged girl, who soon married His stepdad, Joe, who was a total blue-collar guy. He didn't just come to be *like us* so as to save some of us; He became *like the least of us* so as to save all of us. He is not an archetypal king. Instead of ruling from a castle, He had no place to lay His head at night. Instead of overseeing His kingdom from a throne carved out of gold and inlaid with precious jewels, He chose to look out over mankind from a much simpler throne crafted from rough-hewn wooden crossbars. His disciples may have wanted to be first, but He chose to be last—to save them from themselves.

- **WHAT ARE A** few examples of how you think heavenly grandeur will differ from earthly grandeur?

- **IN WHAT WAYS** do you sometimes strive to be first?

- **HOW CAN YOU** specifically fight your inclination to want the seat of glory? How can you "reflect genuine humility" in your spheres of influence?

Day 43

WHEN JUMPSUITS BECOME WINGS

The Spirit of the Lord GOD is on me,
because the LORD has anointed me
to bring good news to the poor.
He has sent me to heal the brokenhearted,
to proclaim liberty to the captives
and freedom to the prisoners;
to proclaim the year of the LORD's favor,
and the day of our God's vengeance;
to comfort all who mourn,
to provide for those who mourn in Zion;
to give them a crown of beauty instead of ashes,
festive oil instead of mourning,
and splendid clothes instead of despair.
And they will be called righteous trees,
planted by the LORD
to glorify him. ISAIAH 61:1–3

ONE OF THE BIGGEST honors and greatest encouragements I've experienced over the past few years has been getting to spend time with an incredible group of men who are seminary students at Angola, one of the largest maximum-security prisons in America. Angola, also known as "The Louisiana State Penitentiary for Men," or "The Farm," or "Alcatraz of the South," used to have the well-deserved reputation as being the bloodiest prison in America—there's several documentaries about it on Netflix.

But not so much anymore. Not in my experience, anyway.

Hope has been palpable to me as I've walked down their prison hallways, or visited the on-property auto shop where inmates restore old cars, or watched inmates-turned-cowboys ride high and proud in their saddles while rounding up the cattle from which come the meat they eat, or tasted fresh vegetables that've just been harvested from their plentiful gardens that same day. That's right, Angola is now reputed to be one of the most self-sustaining prisons in America, requiring significantly less federal funds than others based on comparable numbers of regular population and death row inmates.

The only reason I've had the privilege of spending time with these dear men at Angola is a beautiful, big-hearted, bad-driving, blonde chick named Natalie LaBorde—someone who's become like a baby sister to me and just so happens to be a gifted lawyer and one of the gubernatorial liaisons with the penal system in Louisiana! She'd raved so much about the redemption she was witnessing behind those miles and miles of electrified fence near Cajun country that I asked her if I could tag along with her on a trip. The fact that she wrangled an invitation for me to speak at their seminary—you heard me right—the prison's *seminary* (which is an official extension of New Orleans Baptist Theological Seminary and the first of its kind according to the Department of Corrections) is Nat's typical kind of generous. During later visits, I've had the joy of listening to some of their personal stories (over meals that included beef raised right there in prison pastures) and worshiping with Jesus-loving captives in the campus chapel that was entirely, lovingly, and willingly built by the inmates themselves. All in all, my experiences at Angola have been nothing short of amazing. What I formerly understood about God's mercy has been multiplied there.

During my first visit, I was surprised to find out that many of the students in their seminary are "lifers." That is, they won't ever set foot on ground outside of the Angola compound and therefore won't be eligible for a ministerial job outside of prison. Yet when I asked them why they were working so diligently to complete their coursework, they explained sincerely that they just want to know Jesus at a deeper level and be more effective ambassadors for Him *inside* prison walls. They believe the fruit of spiritual maturity and Gospel effectiveness that comes from studying the Bible will be way more than worth their mental sweat equity. Simply put, they want to know God more and be fruitful *right where they are.*

I'm grateful to now call two gentlemen, in particular, my friends. Between them, they've served almost sixty years in prison. They're both straightforward about their guilt, believe the consequences they're paying for their crimes was deserved based on the very bad and violent choices they made as drug-addicted young men, and both passionately advocate for victim's rights. They've also graduated from New Orleans Baptist Theological Seminary, mentor other inmates—especially those who initially trudged through Angola's gates devoid of hope—and can often be found astride one of Angola's horses, herding cattle and singing a hymn.

They're proof positive that no sin is powerful enough to catapult us beyond the reach of God's grace. Or as my good friend Chris Caine often proclaims passionately in her thick Aussie accent, "Because of *JESUS*, you can start bad and finish good!"

- **WHAT CIRCUMSTANCES OR** relationships that you initially complained to God were too confining, have served to bring about more hope and freedom in your life?

- **HOW DO YOU** resonate with Christine's proclamation about starting bad and finishing good?

- **WHERE HAS GOD** been prompting you to dig in and become more invested for His kingdom's sake?

Day 44
CHRISTIANITY IS NOT A SPECTATOR SPORT

*And let us consider how we may spur one another
on toward love and good deeds.* HEBREWS 10:24 NIV

ONE OF MY FAVORITE activities in the whole world is snow-skiing. I love the feeling of freedom that comes with flying down a steep slope on a cushion of white, sparkling powder. As a matter of fact, I've gotten "chapped throat" several times while skiing because I can't help laughing out of sheer joy when I'm rocketing down a snow-covered hill on twin fiberglass sticks! However, the first time I stood on the top of a mountain in the high country of Colorado wearing a pair of skis, I was much closer to crying than laughing.

Why, you might ask? Because a few of my crazy friends—who had all been ski instructors in college—decided that since I was a decent athlete with daredevil tendencies, we should skip the bunny slopes and head straight to the double black diamond *experts-only* territory on the backside of Vail mountain for my inaugural run.

I can still remember the way fear surged through my mind and body when we got to the edge of the cliff-face they thought I'd have no problem skiing down. My friends began high-fiving each other, giddy about our good fortune of being the first skiers to venture into the back bowls of Vail that morning. Meanwhile I just stood there wide-eyed and mute, imagining myself cartwheeling, completely out of control, several thousand feet down until I splattered on the exposed rocks below. But I didn't want to come across as a sissy-baby, so instead of confessing my apprehension, I simply tried to herd my internal butterflies in the same general direction and focused on not wetting my pants. Especially since the expensive pair I was squeezed into were borrowed and I was pretty sure the owner wouldn't appreciate such a tangible token of my terror.

With whoops and shouts of glee, one right after the other, four of my five so-called-friends leapt off the cliff, executing perfect jump turns in the powdery snow, down the almost-vertical slope until they were wee dots below. One by one they vanished, until my best friend Judy and I were the only ones left at the top. Judy then calmly gave me three tips:

Keep your shoulders square, facing the bottom of the hill.

When making a turn, swivel your hips but keep the rest of your body positioned toward the bottom of the hill.

To initiate a turn, put your weight on the outside edge of the ski you want to turn in the direction of and press down on the little toe of that foot, as well as the big toe of the opposite foot.

After which she smiled as if she'd just explained the easiest task in the world instead of directions regarding hurtling through space. I couldn't decide whether to smile back or punch her in the neck. *What in the heck was an "edge"? How exactly did one "swivel" their hips since as a Christian single woman, that's not an extracurricular activity I'm familiar with? How was I supposed to distinguish between my big toes and little toes while flailing down a mountainside, especially since all ten were numb, frozen stubs by now?*

Given my open mouth and arched eyebrows, I guess the shock and confusion clearly registered because Judy chuckled. Then she took ahold of my elbow, helped me shuffle to the precipice at the top of the ski run and said, "Just point your skis toward the bottom, Lease, and *go!*"

So I did. And it was a total blast! Mind you, I rolled more than I stayed upright for the first two or three hundred yards. But the snow provided a soft cushion for crash landings and by the time we got to the bottom, I couldn't wait to go back to the top and do it all over again.

I think young, stuck, or jaded Christ-followers need a Judy in their lives, too. Don't you? Someone who'll usher them to the top of the radical-Christian-living hill and say, "Now just point your hearts toward Jesus and *go!*"

- **WHAT'S YOUR GREATEST** hesitancy when it comes to "jumping off the cliff" into a more radical Christian life? What are you in danger of losing if you jump?

- **WHO IS A** Judy in your life, someone who spurs you on toward Jesus and challenges you to jump? If you don't have a Judy, how could you take some steps to find one?

- **WHO ARE YOU** being a Judy for in their Christian walk right now?

Day 45
A KING IN COMMONER'S CLOTHES

They came to an area called Gethsemane. Jesus told his disciples, "Sit here while I pray." He took Peter, James, and John with him. He plunged into a sinkhole of dreadful agony. He told them, "I feel bad enough right now to die. Stay here and keep vigil with me." Going a little ahead, he fell to the ground and prayed for a way out: "Papa, Father, you can—can't you?—get me out of this. Take this cup away from me. But please, not what I want—what do you want?" MARK 14:32–36 MSG

AT A RECENT DINNER party with several good friends from church—many of whom are also big talkers and loud laughers like me—someone suggested that we go around the table and share our most embarrassing moments. We all had some pretty cringe-worthy, yet funny train wrecks with which to entertain our fellow diners. In the end, though, Scott Hamilton (who's best known for being an Olympic gold medalist but his true claim to fame is marrying Tracie, one of the kindest, most compassionate women in the entire world who just so happens to be one of my closest friends!) took home the top prize.

Scott began his story with the dry statement, "Okay, first of all I'm a short, bald man who used to wear leotards, so there's that!" I mean, you *know* a good story is coming when that's the opening line. Then he went on to paint the scene. It was a sold-out ice show that took place in a huge arena not long after he'd won the Olympic gold medal in men's figure skating at Sarajevo in 1984. Of course he was the star of the show, so his introduction rivaled that of a king; huge spotlights were illuminated, fog rolled across the floor of the rink, the music swelled to a crescendo, and then Scott came gliding into the light holding a dramatic pose and wearing a skin-tight Superman costume complete with billowing cape. He said the roar of the crowd was so loud it practically held him up during the first triple jump in his program so he couldn't help thinking, *Man, I am SO on tonight!*

However, that packed-to-capacity, cheering-their-guts-out audience also generated a lot of heat. Whether it was simply the warmth of all those bodies, or the hot breaths they were letting out upon each scream and cheer, the heat caused a thin layer of water to form on top of the ice. Which, of course, threw the reigning men's-world-figure-skating champion just a hair off balance as he launched into his next gravity-defying leap. Which, in turn, caused him to catch both toe picks on the landing. And because toe picks stuck in ice act like a hinge, Scott then belly-flopped unceremoniously to the ice with the resounding wet smack of a hooked fish being slapped on the bow of a bass boat just prior to being filleted by some happy angler! Adding insult to injury, when he gamely hopped up to finish the rest of the routine, he looked down to see the watery crash had left a large, very noticeable circular stain on his pants, leaving him looking less like Superman and more like a little boy who'd just wet his pants!

By the end of Scott's hilariously re-enacted, self-effacing story, we were all laughing so hard we were in danger of having some wet-pants accidents of our own!

But then the conversation took a more serious turn, and we talked about how a hero who stumbles is so much more likable than one who appears infallible. Now please, please hear me: I. Do. Not. Believe. King. Jesus. Is. Anything. Less. Than. Perfect. *Our Creator Redeemer is not flawed in any way.* He didn't ever stumble in the ways we do when it comes to sin. However, His agonizing prayer for relief in the garden of Gethsemane definitely makes Him seem more approachable. He may not have sinned, but Jesus knew what it was like for things to feel full of pressure, or even daunting. His ministry (and His cross!) tells us that He knows what it's like to experience the ridicule of onlookers in moments of weakness. In fact, He *chose* to do this—to experience shame before the world and the Father—all for us! So we wouldn't have to! Which makes him a Hero imminently worthy of worshiping, but also safe enough to scoot next to.

- **OVER AND OVER** again the Bible reveals that Jesus is both perfectly holy and perfectly accessible. Which facet of His character are you more comfortable with?

- **HOW DOES IT** encourage you that Jesus has felt the shame of onlookers on your behalf?

- **HOW DOES THIS** change the way you might handle moments you fall in front of others?

Day 46
HURLING LOVE RIGHT BACK

The one who says he is in the light but hates his brother or sister is in the darkness until now. The one who loves his brother or sister remains in the light, and there is no cause for stumbling in him. But the one who hates his brother or sister is in the darkness, walks in the darkness, and doesn't know where he's going, because the darkness has blinded his eyes. 1 JOHN 2:9–11

SEVERAL YEARS AGO, I sold Missy's favorite motorcycle, which was a huge yellow Honda with an "adoption rocks" sidecar, personalized just for her. I sold it because one day while we were cruising down a country road, two young men in a truck flying a large rebel flag from their tailgate pulled up next to us and started hurling not only Coke cans at us, but expletives with the "n" word.

I stared straight ahead and slowed down, praying they'd pass us quickly, especially in light of how vulnerable we were on a motorcycle. Instead, they veered directly in front of us, forcing me to crash our motorcycle into the ditch. By the grace of God, we weren't physically injured, but I knew my little girl's heart was deeply wounded. So as soon as we were able to get the bike out of the ditch and limp home, I sat her in front of me on the couch and said, "Baby, I want to talk to you about what just happened with those guys in the truck." She replied with sad bewilderment, "Why were they so mean to us, Mama?"

She was only six. I thought I'd have more time to explain the ugly and evil reality of racism. A lump formed in my throat as I took both of her tiny hands in mine and said, "Honey, some people have really little lives. They only hang around with other people who look like them and talk like them and think like them. And sometimes, when you choose to live a really little life, your heart and mind get smaller too because they don't have room to grow."

I was then going to warn my beautiful Haitian daughter about how we need to be prepared and alert when we find ourselves in certain, potentially dangerous environments, but she interrupted me and exclaimed brightly, "I know what we need to do, Mama, we need to help their hearts get bigger!"

I've had to have many more similar, increasingly candid, conversations about prejudice, bigotry, and xenophobia with Missy in the years since that terrible day due to the national and world events she sees on television and even what she overhears in school. But the good news is Missy's philosophy hasn't wavered. She continually encourages me to help shriveled hearts get bigger. Somehow my kid sees what some adults and even a contingency of the church seems blind to. That is: hating other image-bearers—even the ones who hate you—is the antithesis of the Gospel.

- **HOW INTENTIONAL ARE** you about loving people who don't look, talk, think, or even worship like you?

- **HOW DO YOU** usually handle the moments when hatred is hurled at you?

- **HOW DID JESUS** help your shriveled heart get bigger? What might it look like for you, like Him, to help someone else's shriveled heart get bigger?

Day 47
WHEN REGULAR ROMEOS JUST WON'T DO

Don't be deceived, my dear brothers and sisters.
Every good and perfect gift is from above, coming down from
the Father of lights, who does not change like shifting shadows. JAMES 1:16–17

VALENTINE'S DAY TENDS TO be a bust in my life. Well, not a complete bust now, because sweet Missy always makes me a card asking me to be her Valentine. I didn't used to be sentimental about saving cards, but now that I have a tender-hearted daughter, every single one she gives me goes into a special box that would be one of the things I'd try to tote out with me (along with her, of course, and my Bible) if our log home ever caught on fire!

Anyway, my little girl's affection is definitely no small thing, but dang, sometimes I wish there was some handsome beau with a card in one hand, a fistful of roses in the other, and a lovesick grin standing outside the door to my heart on that one day in February each year when red hearts seem to proliferate the globe and every Hallmark, Target, Walgreens, and Publix I walk in goads shoppers to buy something for that "special person" in your life.

Now I do have a cadre of older, single girlfriends who've rechristened February 14th "Galentine's Day," and they always graciously invite me to their estrogen-filled soiree that evening. But alas, normally I turn to other people for comfort: namely, Ben and Jerry, and their chocolate peanut butter concoction of pure goodness.

However, during the first week of February this year I remembered that the onslaught of romantic love cards and tchotchkes and social media memes was right around the corner and I did something more productive. I went out and picked my own boyfriend and decided to memorize a love letter he wrote. Well, he's actually only a pretend boyfriend, plus he died a really, really long time ago and was happily married, so my ardor is unrequited. Also, it's a sermon, not a love letter, that I've been memorizing. But I'll be darned if the following words Charles Spurgeon preached well over a century ago didn't smooth over the Valentine's Day divot in my heart:

"Remember God is the same, whatever is removed. Your friends may be disaffected, your ministers may be taken away, every thing may change, but God does not. Your brethren may change and cast out your name as vile: but God will love you still. Let your station in life change, and your property be gone; let your whole life be shaken, and you become weak and sickly; let everything flee away—there is one place where change cannot put his finger; there is one name on which mutability can never be written; there is one heart which never can alter; that heart is God's—that name Love." —Charles Spurgeon[10]

Dr. Spurgeon's sermon is 165 or so years old now yet it continues to resonate deeply in the human heart because while most of us recognize change is inevitable, we still long for a love relationship that is secure enough for us to attach our hope to it without fear it will falter or ultimately fizzle out. We long for a *real* Romeo—one who will be true-blue, whose love will remain constant no matter what. And contrary to what Valentine's Cards proclaim, our Creator-Redeemer is the only One who fits that description. His unconditional love for us is the only type that will not vacillate one bit.

So whether a special handsome beau gives you red roses and a box of gourmet chocolates on February 14th or you end up watching a sappy romantic comedy in your sweatpants with a pint of ice cream, know this: when you put your hope in Jesus Christ, YOU became the object of *God's* affection, and His perfect, infinite love for you will never, ever fade or fail!

- **IS THERE A** day or season that corresponds with the feeling of loneliness for you?

- **WHAT ARE YOU** intentionally doing to prepare your heart beforehand?

- **HOW HAVE YOU** run away from God during this hard season instead of toward Him?

Day 48

THE GALVANIZING GRACE OF GLANCING BACK

Long ago God spoke to our ancestors by the prophets at different times and in different ways. In these last days, he has spoken to us by his Son. God has appointed him heir of all things and made the universe through him. The Son is the radiance of God's glory and the exact expression of his nature, sustaining all things by his powerful word. After making purification for sins, he sat down at the right hand of the Majesty on high. HEBREWS 1:1–3

LONG AGO GOD SPOKE through super-smart prophet dudes like Isaiah and Elijah—who were incredibly engaging messengers even though they didn't have the luxury of PowerPoint presentations or YouTube clips or fog machines. God also spoke through signs and dreams, which are effectively Insta-storied in the lives of Daniel and Job. He used a flaming topiary to communicate with Moses.

Some even thought God spoke through the "Urim and Thummim," which were basically holy dice used to discern His will. Remember how the disciples "cast lots" to replace Judas at the beginning of Acts? Theological consensus is the disciples used Urim and Thummim in that situation. Which has a weird Vegas vibe, doesn't it?

But after the author of Hebrews tells us that God spoke at different *times* (*polymeros* in the original language) and in different *ways* (*polytropos*), we get to the interesting and oh-so-significant phrase in verse 2: *In these last days.* Fun fact: When the *last* or *latter days* is specified in the New Testament, it's referring to the time period between the first and second coming of Jesus Christ. It's what Peter was preaching about at Pentecost when he quoted Joel and said God would pour out His Spirit in the *last days* (Acts 2:17).

So, just like the audience of the book of Hebrews and the audience of Peter's sermon, we too are living in the "already but not yet" times—the times where humanity has *already* witnessed the first coming of Jesus Christ, but hasn't yet seen the second one. So, if you've put your hope in His sacrificial death on the cross and subsequent resurrection, there are parts of your Christian walk that are a done deal. They've already happened. They are in the "already" phase. For example, you are *already* reconciled to God. The debt of your sin has been completely paid for.

However, here's the "not yet" part. There are things still to come. For example, we are *not yet* glorified. This spinning planet is not our home. One day Jesus will come a second time; He'll split the sky wide open while riding a white horse and He'll escort us—His bride—to a new heaven and earth, where there will be no more dying and no more crying, and the world will run as it was always meant to!

Meanwhile, much like those Jewish Christians the book of Hebrews was originally written to in the first century (a time and place when Christ-followers were being severely persecuted), we find that there's way too much dying and crying here on earth, don't we? We find that our lives are sometimes super-hard. Family members might poke fun of us when we pray before the Thanksgiving meal. Coworkers might marginalize us as being narrow-minded hatemongers after they discover that we believe the Bible is true. Sometimes the fact that we stick out like sore thumbs in secular culture might make us feel like throwing in the Gospel towel, too. While these things aren't the exact same persecution ancient believers had to endure, they are costs. And we feel them. Every single time.

The good news is that even though we're living in a broken world instead of Eden, we do have the testimony of the Son during these last days. The one and only begotten Son of God the Father. The Lamb of God. The Bright Morning Star. The Lily of the Valley. JESUS! So why settle for prophets, burning shrubbery, or dice when you can have direct access to the Prince of Peace?

When the going gets tougher than usual, let's make a pact to look back on what Jesus already accomplished for us on the cross and then lean fully into the supernatural reality of His outstretched arms. Those backward glances and lingering embraces are what will give us the grace we need to forge ahead with fresh faith. We will get to the "not yet" Jesus promises in due time. And the fuel we need to get there is in the "already" that He's given us.

- **HOW DID YOUR** heart respond when you first believed that Jesus Christ is the Son of God and He loves YOU?

- **HOW DO YOU** typically try to hear from God? How does this passage in Hebrews encourage or challenge that approach?

- **HOW MIGHT YOUR** life look different if you prioritized time in your weekly schedule to "glance back" at what Christ has already done for you?

Day 49
THE DANCE OF THE DELIGHTED-IN

Hallelujah!
Sing to the LORD a new song,
his praise in the assembly of the faithful.
Let Israel celebrate its Maker;
let the children of Zion rejoice in their King.
Let them praise his name with dancing
and make music to him with tambourine and lyre.
For the LORD takes pleasure in his people;
he adorns the humble with salvation.
Let the faithful celebrate in triumphal glory;
let them shout for joy on their beds. PSALM 149:1–5

———

EVEN THOUGH MISSY HAS me for a mom—a rhythm-challenged chick who was raised in a mostly non-boogying church tradition—she's never met a sanctuary she wasn't comfortable cutting a rug in! And despite moves that would make most observers wince, I'm inclined to join her at this age and stage of life! I guess my Dad Harper's Pentecostal DNA has finally crowded out the non-wiggly, pantyhose-clad part I inherited from my mother's side of the family!

Thankfully, First Baptist in downtown Houston (where we had the gift of visiting recently) was filled with welcoming image-bearers who wrapped my joyful, dancing girl into their collective embrace when we recently worshiped Immanuel—God *with* us and *for* us—together! I'm so incredibly grateful for communities of faith who reflect the inclusive kindness of King Jesus. Because of the wonderfully unique and wildly gracious church communities we've had the honor of visiting over the years, my little girl's understanding of "church" is a safe place filled with all kinds of people—most of them smiling and friendly— where she's free to express her delight in Christ. Unlike me, who grew up associating church more so with solemnity, uncomfortable shoes, and ethnic homogeny than with unbridled joy, genuine affection for Jesus, and a beauti- fully diverse crew of congregants who sing His name together.

Maybe the house of worship you call home leans toward formality with gleaming pews, stained glass windows, and a robe-wearing spiritual leader.

Or perhaps your family of faith is more of an informal place with coffee in the lobby, theater-style seating, and a pastor who wears torn jeans and sports tattoos. No matter what form it takes, I hope it's a warm setting where children and adults aren't all exactly alike, apart from their common sense of feeling free to dance. At least in the privacy of their own hearts!

- **WHEN AND WHERE** do you feel the most liberated when it comes to expressing your love for Jesus?

- **WHAT DOES PASSION** for God look like in your life?

- **WHO MIGHT NEED** to be welcomed into your church community the way Missy was welcomed in this story?

Day 50
WELL SHUT MY MOUTH

Then the Lord *answered Job from the whirlwind. He said:*
Who is this who obscures my counsel
with ignorant words?
Get ready to answer me like a man;
when I question you, you will inform me.
Where were you when I established the earth?
Tell me, if you have understanding.
Who fixed its dimensions? Certainly you know! JOB 38:1–5

WE'VE SPENT ENOUGH TIME together at this point for you to pick up on the fact that I'm a bit of a mama bear when it comes to my daughter Missy. And when someone threatens my cub, well, I sometimes overreact a *teensy* bit. As was the case a few years ago when I had an exploratory conversation with an administrator at a private Christian school I was considering enrolling her in. About midway through the conversation, when she was dutifully explaining their policy regarding students taking prescription meds on school property for medical conditions like diabetes or asthma, I told her that Missy didn't need to take meds during the school day because I administered her HIV meds at home.

At which point this lady looked at me completely flabbergasted, then replied nervously, "I wasn't aware your daughter had HIV." I said, "Yes ma'am, she does. Although by the grace of God the virus is completely undetectable in her bloodstream, which is much like being in remission if you have cancer or leukemia." After quietly digesting that information for a few seconds, she asked soberly, "But what if she cuts her head at school and it starts bleeding?"

Even though I could feel my blood starting to heat up, I answered very calmly and rationally, "Well, then according to state law you'd treat her like you would any other student or teacher who had a bleeding wound, you'd glove first and then apply a bandage. Or if it was a real gusher, you'd apply pressure, call 911 then call me."

I promise I was willing to give her the benefit of the doubt—the true facts about HIV often take some time to learn—that is, until she lowered her boom of ignorance by asking, "But what if one of the other students eats off her plate at lunchtime?" I took a deep breath to make sure my tone was non-combative and my expression was friendly before responding, "You know it would probably help for me to explain how HIV is transmitted."

Then I leaned a little closer and explained in *very graphic sexual terms* how the virus is most commonly transmitted, and must confess I rather enjoyed watching her eyes widen and red splotches begin to appear on her face and neck. I finished with a flourish adding, "Oh and lastly, there's IV drug use—for instance when people shoot heroine with shared, dirty needles. But since I don't think any of those activities are permitted at your school and since there's never been a reported incident of HIV being transmitted through casual contact like sharing lunch or a kiss or even sitting on the same toilet seat, there's really no chance that my daughter's illness could be considered contagious in this environment. As a matter of fact, statistically speaking, it's more likely that one of your students will be eaten by a Great White Shark right here in landlocked Tennessee than 'catch' HIV from my kid."

There was such a long silence following my vivid (albeit medically accurate) explanation that I finally interjected perkily, "You know, I believe the best way we can eradicate the stigma surrounding HIV is through open communication and on-going education so I'd be happy to share this information at the next parents' meeting!" At which point she *blurted*, "Oh no, NO Miss Harper, that won't be necessary!"

I still get tickled when I think about her stupefied expression, and now her face is the image I see when I read Job's response to God's lecture. I mean, mere moments before this response from God, Job had been stomping around, waving his fist at heaven and demanding an audience with the Creator of the Universe. And then, upon God lowering the boom, he changes his tune and responds ever so meekly:

> "I'm speechless, in awe—words fail me.
> I should never have opened my mouth!
> I've talked too much, way too much.
> I'm ready to shut up and listen." (Job 40:3–5 MSG)

- **WHEN HAS GOD** interrupted you lately—effectively shutting your mouth in the middle of a complaint—and reminded you that you actually aren't in charge of the universe?

- **WHY DO WE** sometimes need forthright reminders from God about His power and control instead of subtle hints?

- **HOW DO YOU** usually respond in your heart when God shuts your mouth?

HOLY MOSES

After six days Jesus took Peter, James, and John and led them up a high mountain by themselves to be alone. He was transfigured in front of them, and his clothes became dazzling—extremely white as no launderer on earth could whiten them. Elijah appeared to them with Moses, and they were talking with Jesus. MARK 9:2–4

THROUGHOUT ALL MY CHILDHOOD years in Sunday school, high school years in youth group, college years in Campus Life and Fellowship of Christian Athletes meetings, and early adult years in women's Bible studies, it secretly bugged me that God didn't allow Moses to enter Canaan. I know Isaiah says that we can't fully comprehend God's sovereign actions because His ways are as high above ours as the heavens are above the earth (Isa. 55:8–9), and I know Moses deserved *some* kind of time-out after losing his temper and whacking that rock and all (Num. 20). But revoking his Promised Land ticket seemed way too harsh to me.

I mean, good night, didn't it count for something that the poor dude had risked his life to confront that cruelly oppressive Pharaoh, then had bravely led the Israelites out of slavery, *and* had worked his tail off leading all those rebellious, prone-to-grumble ragamuffins for forty years in the wilderness? Of course, I didn't confess my covert grudge in small group or anything because I didn't want to be judged, but I sure chafed at the fact that poor Moe got buried on Mt. Nebo and didn't get to set one foot in the land of promise he'd worked so hard to get to.

But then one day about twenty years ago, I was studying Mark chapter 9 and it hit me like a ton of beautiful bricks: the transfiguration took place on one of the mountains on the northern shore of the Sea of Galilee. Some New Testament scholars think this glowing miracle took place on Mt. Hermon, but regardless of whether it happened on the top of Mt. Hermon or an adjacent hill, what's *definite* is that the transfiguration took place on a scenic point smack-dab in the middle of Canaan! Which means, Moses *did* make it to the land of milk and honey after all! Even though he didn't get to make his entrance marching through the Jordan on dry ground with Joshua and the second generation of wilderness sojourners, a few centuries later—*long* after his physical death—good old Moe still got to stand in the Promised Land, wearing his glorified body and surely grinning from ear to ear because he was standing right next to the illuminated Messiah! He didn't just get to see it. He got to see it with *Jesus* beside him. God wanted to stand next to him, right there in the flesh, and take it in *with* him.

Wowzaroonie—what a jaw-drop-inducing, biblical reminder that our Creator-Redeemer is *not* bound by time and space! That when it feels like He's not hearing our prayers because we aren't getting immediate answers, He's still moving mountains on our behalf.

Romans 8:28 isn't hyperbolic . . . everything *will* work out for our good and His glory ultimately. It just might not coincide with where we've currently got it scheduled on our calendar.

- **WHAT REQUEST HAVE** you made to God that He seems to be taking an especially long time responding to?

- **DO YOU THINK** waiting has made you bitter or better? Why?

- **HOW DOES MOSES'** story here encourage you in the waiting?

Day 52

SOMETIMES GROUP HUGS HURT

"If the world hates you, understand that it hated me before it hated you. If you were of the world, the world would love you as its own. However, because you are not of the world, but I have chosen you out of it, the world hates you. Remember the word I spoke to you: 'A servant is not greater than his master.' If they persecuted me, they will also persecute you. If they kept my word, they will also keep yours." JOHN 15:18–20

I WAS IN A church setting recently where a female leader asked all the moms to stand up. Then she proclaimed in a sing-song tone how wonderful it was that we had husbands who worked hard so that we could all stay home and focus on raising our children. After which, she asked all the "hubbies" to stand up and lay hands on their "wifeys" in prayer. It took every shred of discipline I have not to bellow over the crowd of bowed heads that I've been praying for a baby daddy who would love my adopted daughter with all his heart and lay his hands all over me for a long time, but it just hasn't happened yet!

Strong Christian women—whether we're homeschool moms, Harvard-educated attorneys, or both—need to understand that not-fitting-in is part of our job description. The world, and sometimes even the prevailing Christian culture we're plopped in, won't necessarily agree with—much less applaud—the game plan God has given us *personally* to carry out. But we must do it anyway. Because godly obedience isn't about being patted on the back or enveloped in a group hug. Plus, this supernatural love story called the Bible makes it crystal clear that homogeny and popularity are both overrated.

In fact, there are multiple passages in the Old Testament and New Testament describing God's people as aliens, strangers, or sojourners in this world. In other words, *we aren't supposed to fit!* We're supposed to reflect the steadfast character of Christ—not the cheesy paradigm of perky church ladies nor the fleeting inclinations of pop culture.

Plus, don't forget Jesus wasn't the kind of social butterfly who tried to win the admiration or belonging of every room He entered, either. In fact, more of His thirty-three years on this planet were spent as an outsider, not an insider.

- **WHERE DO YOU** feel most like an outsider in Christian subculture?

- **WHERE MIGHT GOD** be calling you that risks your sense of belonging to the "in crowd" of certain social circles?

- **WHY DO YOU** think Jesus didn't need the approval of these sorts of social circles?

Day 53

NEAR ENOUGH TO KNOW WHOSE WHISPER

"My sheep hear my voice, I know them, and they follow me. I give them eternal life, and they will never perish. No one will snatch them out of my hand." JOHN 10:27–28

WE MOVED INTO A new house with a pool when Missy was five and didn't know how to swim yet. Because I worked as a lifeguard in Florida when I was growing up and have been privy to one too many drownings and near-drownings, I'm passionate about protecting kids around water. However, the swimming lessons Missy had taken the summer before our move hadn't helped much, so I decided to teach her some basic water safety principles a couple of months after we moved in, as soon as the ice on top of our cement pond melted!

A few minutes after I began the very first lesson, while Missy and I were still standing safely on the "sun-shelf" (a raised area for sunbathing) in only a few inches of water, I realized I'd forgotten the sunscreen. So I said, "Hang on just a minute, honey, I'll be right back," then turned around and jogged up the stairs that lead from our pool deck to the porch where we keep the sunscreen. To this day, I don't know why I did something so foolish and potentially dangerous. I *know better* than take my eyes off a child who can't swim near water—even for a few seconds. Which is all it took for the unthinkable to happen.

In the ten or so seconds it took me to reach the sunscreen basket twenty feet away on the porch, Missy got intrigued by a leaf floating past, and when she scooted to the edge of the sun-shelf to try to grab it, she slipped and fell into water that was way over her precious little head. Of course, I didn't see any of this happen because I stupidly had my back to my baby girl. And it all happened so fast that she didn't scream in fear or call out for help. She just made the tiniest of yips as she went under. It was less than a whisper, a barely noticeable blip. But that sliver of a sound wave hit my ears like a charge of dynamite and I knew instinctively what had happened.

I whirled around, grabbed the handrail, vaulted over the entire flight of steps to the deck and dove into the pool in what seemed to be one single, superhuman motion. I had her up and out of the water in a flash, before she had time to gulp water or get scared. She just looped her arms around my neck and smiled, as if it had all been one grand adventure. I didn't let myself sob until she was dried off and happily stretched out on the couch under a blanket watching *Paw Patrol.*

Of course, we stayed in the pool the next day until our lips turned blue and I was sure that Missy could make it to the edge if she ever fell in again. And within another week or two her mermaid skills emerged, and she became an excellent swimmer. But I'll never forget that close call and how that faintest of sounds Missy made when she slipped under water captured my attention. I believe I was able to hear her because I'd spent so many hours, on so many nights, standing over her bed, just listening to her breathe while she slept after I brought her home from Haiti. I'd already spent so much time in the quiet company of this undeserved miracle child of mine, that her softest cry registered like a car horn in my mother's ears.

I think that's how it's supposed to be with us and Jesus, too. We should be able to *hear Him* because we've spent so much time *near Him.*

- **WHAT IS THE** most common kind of static in your heart and mind that keeps you from hearing God clearly?

- **HOW CAN YOU** prioritize spending more time near the Lord—not as a task to check off, but as a way to better know His voice when He's guiding you?

- **WHOSE VOICE DO** you know like the back of your hand? How does it feel to know God wants you to know His voice this intimately?

Day 54
CHOOSE HOPE

And regarding the question, friends, that has come up about what happens to those already dead and buried, we don't want you in the dark any longer. First off, you must not carry on over them like people who have nothing to look forward to, as if the grave were the last word. Since Jesus died and broke loose from the grave, God will most certainly bring back to life those who died in Jesus. 1 THESSALONIANS 4:13–14 MSG

I REMEMBER ALL TOO well those very long, hard, heartbreaking days that followed my brother-in-law James's tragic and unexpected death (which occurred only a month after COVID-19 was declared a global pandemic and it seemed the entire planet was already grappling with some measure of grief and anxiety). Of course, his loss is still acute for all of us who knew and loved him, but the initial impact was brutal. Every morning, I'd wake up to the immediate, terrible memory of his death . . . it was like being hit by a wave of sorrow every time you break the surface for a breath of air after being underwater for so long you thought your lungs would burst. I couldn't imagine what my sister and nephews were going through in the wake of his loss. The fact that I couldn't do very much—besides listen—to lessen their grief in those first few weeks compounded my sadness.

However, as I slowly ambled around the yard early one morning during that initial season of grief, I sensed a quiet pulse of hope in my heavy heart. The peach trees I had planted just a few years ago (to camouflage the big, ugly, pokey-outy green top of a giant submerged propane tank) was now laden with hundreds, maybe thousands, of peaches. The smell was heavenly. Tiny apples had sprouted from the white flowers that covered our apple trees only a few weeks before, and green plums looked like they were playing hide-and-seek throughout our mini-orchard because they were the exact same color of the leaves. Tomatoes and blackberries and blueberries and strawberries and herbs all seemed to be shouting happily for attention—"Hey y'all, look at how big we're getting!"—while the irises and roses and lavender and jasmine performed a collective wave of blooms in appreciation of their fruity cousins. And all at once, I found myself remembering afresh how the austere barrenness of winter serves to make the abundant growth of spring all the more glorious.

Yes, we live in a broken world that is marred by gut-wrenching loss and great grief and global pandemics, but God's compassionate presence is never absent no matter how dark or difficult the season. Because of what Jesus accomplished on that Resurrection Sunday over two thousand year ago, death does not have the final say. Life does. Therefore, we really don't have to grieve as those who have no hope. We can choose hope and speak life and love hard, even when it is hard.

- **HOW HAVE YOU** experienced God's presence and comfort in the wintery seasons of your life?

- **WHAT KINDS OF** grief or loss still wash over you like a wave sometimes?

- **WHAT MIGHT IT** look like to grieve in these moments with hope?

MY DAD RULES

All the nations you have made will come and worship before you, Lord; they will bring glory to your name. For you are great and do marvelous deeds; you alone are God. Teach me your way, LORD, that I may rely on your faithfulness; give me an undivided heart, that I may fear your name. PSALM 86:9–11 NIV

ONE OF MY FAVORITE movies of all times is *To Kill a Mockingbird* (based on Harper Lee's classic novel of the same name, which was published in 1960). The storyline is based on a tough-on-the-outside-tender-on-the-inside attorney by the name of Atticus Finch (played by Gregory Peck). Atticus is basically limping gruffly through life—with his two young children skipping warily behind him—in the aftermath of his wife's untimely death. But then he makes a life-changing choice that ultimately transforms his fractured little family. He decides to become the defense attorney for an innocent black man named Tom, who's been framed for raping a white girl in their small, Southern, segregated town.

My favorite scene in the film takes place soon after Tom is convicted, even though everyone in the courtroom knows he's not guilty—especially after the impeccable, impassioned defense Atticus has presented. Nonetheless, the all-white jury blindly chooses tradition over truth and unfairly hands down a guilty verdict. Bigoted hooligans whoop with glee when the verdict is read, while all the black people overlooking from the balcony (because the main floor of the courthouse was for "whites only") react in stunned silence. The bottom floor of the courtroom quickly empties as boisterous white men file out, slapping each other on the back in congratulations.

Throughout all the downstairs commotion, those in the balcony remained seated, shocked, and deeply disappointed that Tom—who'd by now become a symbol for anyone with brown skin in their community—had been unfairly accused and convicted simply because of his race. Then the camera pans to Atticus. To the only white man who'd behaved honorably that day by insisting that *all* people deserved to be treated with fairness and dignity regardless of their color or creed. It's obvious by the sag of his shoulders that he's broken-hearted over the verdict, too. He methodically gathers his papers from the defendant's table, puts them into his briefcase, then turns to walk out of the courtroom. And that's when people in the balcony began standing up. First one by one, then dozens of them.

At which point, a kindly old pastor taps Atticus's precocious seven-year-old daughter, Jean Louise (whose nickname is "Scout") on the shoulder. Scout had chosen to sit up in the balcony throughout the trial and in that particular moment is plopped on the floor with her tomboyish legs dangling through the balusters. The pastor instructs her fondly but firmly, "Miss Jean Louis, stand up. Your father's passing." She glances up questionably but once she realizes the entire balcony is standing out of respect for her father, her countenance transforms from that of a wary little girl to one whose heart has begun to beat for her daddy. She scrambles quickly to her feet and stretches as tall as she can so as to show her esteem for her father too.

I think I've cried every time I've watched that scene of Scout standing up, and something deep in my heart stirs. Because I want to be found standing wide-eyed with reverence for my Father, too. And not because He merely tries to achieve vindication for those He loves, but because ultimately He *always* achieves it!

- **WHAT'S MORE NATURAL** for you: feeling awed because of the hugeness and holiness of God or feeling safe because of the compassion of God?

- **HOW DO YOU** think reverence for God and intimacy with God best coexist?

- **WHAT TYPICALLY HOLDS** you back from "standing wide-eyed with reverence" for your heavenly Father?

Day 56
IF YOU DON'T HAVE SOMETHING GOOD TO SAY . . .

The LORD hates six things; in fact, seven are detestable to him: arrogant eyes, a lying tongue, hands that shed innocent blood, a heart that plots wicked schemes, feet eager to run to evil, a lying witness who gives false testimony, and one who stirs up trouble among brothers. PROVERBS 6:16–19

No foul language should come from your mouth, but only what is good for building up someone in need, so that it gives grace to those who hear. EPHESIANS 4:29

Don't criticize one another, brothers and sisters. Anyone who defames or judges a fellow believer defames and judges the law. If you judge the law, you are not a doer of the law but a judge. JAMES 4:11

A FRIEND RECENTLY SENT me a few blogs and websites—ones in which confessing Christians are spending lots of time and energy disparaging other Christ-followers. One of them even boasted a public list of "false prophets" that included my name, and it broke my heart. Not because I was accused of being a false prophet (frankly, I was thrilled to be included on a list that was filled with many godly women I love and respect), but because another precious image-bearer was choosing to live such a small, embittered life spewing judgment and sewing discord instead of living the abundant, preferring-others-for-the-sake-of-the-Gospel kind of life Jesus died to provide for us.

I can't help wondering how much it grieves our Redeemer when we spend more time eviscerating each other for having minor doctrinal differences than we do exulting about the unconditional love of Jesus Christ that saved our sorry behinds, sharing the living hope of the Gospel with the wounded world around us, and caring for the poor and marginalized. Therefore, it did my heart especially good in the days that followed to visit a wonderful church in Mississippi with a bunch of women from very diverse ethnic and denominational backgrounds, all worshiping the One true God, King JESUS, who is a *friend of sinners*! May we all follow their lead and major on the majors in this life, uniting together to praise our King while we still have breath in our lungs. Selah.

- **WHAT PERCENTAGE OF** words that fall out of your mouth—or through your fingers on social media—would you estimate give grace to those who hear them?

- **WHAT USUALLY TRIGGERS** you to use your speech for discord or quarreling instead of encouragement and edification?

- **HOW CAN YOU** better prepare for this trigger so that you are ready the next time it pops up in your life?

Day 57

MULES AT THE KENTUCKY DERBY

The angel of the LORD came, and he sat under the oak that was in Ophrah, which belonged to Joash, the Abiezrite. His son Gideon was threshing wheat in the winepress in order to hide it from the Midianites. Then the angel of the LORD appeared to him and said, "The LORD is with you, valiant warrior." Gideon said to him, "Please, my lord, if the LORD is with us, why has all this happened? And where are all his wonders that our ancestors told us about? They said, 'Hasn't the LORD brought us out of Egypt?' But now the LORD has abandoned us and handed us over to Midian." The LORD turned to him and said, "Go in the strength you have and deliver Israel from the grasp of Midian. I am sending you!" He said to him, "Please, Lord, how can I deliver Israel? Look, my family is the weakest in Manasseh, and I am the youngest in my father's family." "But I will be with you," the LORD said to him. "You will strike Midian down as if it were one man." JUDGES 6:11–16

IN 1998 I LEFT a great position with an international, para-church ministry called Focus on the Family in Colorado Springs and took a job as the women's director at Christ Presbyterian Church in Nashville, Tennessee. I made this change largely because their lead pastor at the time—Dr. Charles McGowan— ensured I could pursue the seminary training I was yearning for while I was on staff at the church. I also took the church job because I was so impressed with how honorable and gracious Charles was during the interview process. He exuded the kind of safe, paternal kindness that should be found in any senior pastor, all the way down to his gracious way of speaking. And that wasn't just true in the interview. In fact, over the next five years that he was my boss, I never heard an unkind word about someone fall out of his mouth that entire time.

However, at the very beginning of my tenure at the church, I felt like some of his words about me were painting too rosy of a picture. Various times during those first few months, Charles would rave about what a blessing I was from the pulpit. In multiple staff meetings, he'd say how enthused he was about what a great addition I'd made to the team. I finally got so embarrassed by his effusive praise that I scheduled a one-on-one meeting through his secretary to discuss the issue of favoritism. I remember wearing my nicest "church girl" dress to the meeting and being flustered as a long-tailed cat in a room full of rocking chairs, because by then, I already had so much admiration for Charles and didn't want to come across as disrespectful or impertinent.

My voice quivered slightly as I nervously proclaimed something along the lines of, "Charles, thank you very much for your advocacy and warm reception, but you've been so positive about me I'm afraid people are going to get the idea that I have it all together. And I don't." I went on to confess much more than was probably appropriate (don't you sometimes find yourself looking back on your youth and shaking your head at the foolishness you thought was wisdom then?) to prove that I wasn't nearly as ideal as he'd professed publicly. *He has me all wrong, and I'll show him just how far he is off the mark!* For whatever reason, I thought sharing my dirty laundry with the senior pastor who'd hired me to help shepherd his flock was a commendable thing to do. It's a wonder he didn't kick me out of his office with a pink slip containing directions to the nearest unemployment office!

Instead, that dear, wise, godly man patiently waited for me to finish prattling on and on. Then, he took my trembling young hands into his that were gnarled with age, and assured me in an oh-so-kind, fatherly tone, "I'm *so* glad you don't have it all together, Lisa, because if you did God probably wouldn't use you much here."

Dr. McGowan epitomized grace to me. His leadership is one of the big reasons I can now focus on God's transformational compassion more than my considerable weaknesses. And his guidance helped develop my belief that a perfect God really can use a perfect mess like me.

- **WHAT JOB HAS** God called you to do that you feel completely inadequate for?

- **WHO HAS GOD** placed in your life to show you that He is in the business of using your weakness for His glory?

- **WHO IN YOUR** life feels weak in their ministry calling right now? How might you encourage them?

Day 58

BEHOLDING THE LAMB

The soldiers took Jesus into the palace (called Praetorium) and called together the entire brigade. They dressed him up in purple and put a crown plaited from a thornbush on his head. Then they began their mockery: "Bravo, King of the Jews!" They banged on his head with a club, spit on him, and knelt down in mock worship. After they had had their fun, they took off the purple cape and put his own clothes back on him. Then they marched out to nail him to the cross. MARK 15:16–20 MSG

FROM HEARING THE SOUNDS of His dear friends' snores in between His own ragged sobs of grief in Gethsemane to observing the pathetic charade of Pilate's handwashing, Jesus endured a continuum of unjustified infidelity throughout the last few days of His earthly life that would test the character of any man. But of course, He wasn't just *any* man. He is *the Christ*. The Anointed One our heavenly Father commissioned and purposed to receive the punishment we deserve. Which means He wasn't called to simply stand firm in the face of hardship like some skinny but determined freshman at a military school. No, He was called to bend toward betrayal. To lean into the vicious lies being spewed about Him. To humbly accept a completely undeserved capital punishment charge without any kind of appeal. To mute His own omnipotent roar and become the Passover Lamb.

A few years ago, my friend Cheryl, who's the women's ministry director at a large church in Texas, told me she was walking down a church hallway on a weekday when she heard sobs coming from the library. She turned and hurried toward the cries, thinking someone was obviously distraught and needed help. She was surprised to discover that the weeping was coming from one of their missionaries, who was home on furlough for a few months. He and his wife had dedicated their lives to sharing the living hope of Jesus and translating the Bible into the language of a small, largely unreached people group who live in a remote area in West Africa. When she approached him and gently asked if he was okay he responded, "Oh, I'll be okay, Cheryl. It's just that I'm translating the crucifixion."

May we all be so moved by what happened on that very first "Good" Friday. May we all lean into Him, and never forget all that He leaned into for us.

- **LESS THAN A** week before Good Friday, Jesus was hailed as a hero when He entered Jerusalem. What do you think His followers were feeling as they observed this shocking reversal from adulation to degradation?

- **WHAT TEMPTS YOU** to forget all that Christ leaned into for you?

- **HOW WOULD YOU** explain what was happening on the cross to a non-Christian friend?

Day 59

LOOKING HARD OR HARDLY LOOKING

"But from there, you will search for the Lord your God, and you will find him when you seek him with all your heart and all your soul. When you are in distress and all these things have happened to you, in the future you will return to the Lord your God and obey him. He will not leave you, destroy you, or forget the covenant with your ancestors that he swore to them by oath, because the Lord your God is a compassionate God." DEUTERONOMY 4:29–31

DURING MY EARLY THIRTIES I lived in Colorado and loved running in the Rocky Mountains. My favorite route to run was called Pulpit Rock Trail in Palmer Park near where I lived in Colorado Springs; it winds up well over a mile through an evergreen forest and ends in an alpine meadow with this amazing view of Pike's Peak. I went there at least two or three times a week to work out and unwind during those six years I was a mountain girl.

Which is why I was really disappointed toward the end of that season of my life when newspapers and TV stations began reporting about violent crimes that had taken place in Palmer Park. The reports included scary details and grim-faced warnings that women especially should avoid hiking, biking, or running in the park until this particular criminal was apprehended. However, soon after hearing the warnings, we had an absolutely gorgeous fall weekend. The sky was bright blue, the temperature was in the sixties; I thought, *Surely it's too pretty for criminal activity this weekend!*

So, with only optimistic thoughts in my head, I drove to the park that Saturday afternoon. I couldn't help noticing that there was only one other car parked at the trail. And then, when I walked to the trail head to begin my run, I noticed signs from the Colorado Springs Police, clearly warning women not to use the trail system in light of the recent assaults. Of course, I pushed the seed of apprehension aside and jogged right past the signs. I ran my usual route uphill through those majestic Ponderosa Pines and sang worship songs in the crisp mountain air and felt like my soul was sighing contentedly within me because of the mental relaxation that came with stretching my legs in God's beautiful Creation. That is, until I got to the very top of the trail and right before I stepped into my favorite meadow, sitting about fifty feet in front of me was a *naked* man.

I thought, *Oh good night! I can't believe this! Here I was being all spiritual—I was even singing a hymn—and I've run smack into a criminal in his birthday suit!* I felt hotly indignant for a few seconds until it occurred to me that I was in a super-vulnerable position. I hadn't seen anybody else on the trail, the sun was about to set, the area was so remote no one could hear me if I screamed, and I'd left my cell phone in my car.

Now when I get nervous, my mind races like a kid pumped up on sugar and caffeine and I have a hard time thinking clearly. There were only two minimally clear thoughts in my head as I stood there quivering behind a pine tree, hoping the naked man wouldn't notice me:

1. I read somewhere—or maybe watched it on *Oprah*—that men who expose themselves are typically cowards and non-confrontive.
2. I read in a hiking magazine that if you come upon a wild animal in the woods—unless it's a bear—it behooves you to put your hands over your head and advance toward them, all the while speaking in deep guttural tones, which usually intimidates the animal and causes them to run away.

These two thoughts seemed like perfectly rational logic at the time. So, I took a deep breath and jumped out from behind the tree with my hands over my head and ran toward him screaming "Hey!" just as guttural as I could. And it worked, because he looked really startled, then jumped up and began sprinting away from me!

It was only then that I noticed the tiny, blue running shorts he'd obviously been wearing the entire time. You know those short-shorts serious runners sometimes wear that have slits up the side, which splay open when they sit down?

Because of the way that guy was sitting and the fact that my sight line was partly obscured by a tree, I could've *sworn* he was naked! But then I got so tickled watching him run away from me because he kept looking back over his shoulder, obviously worried that I was going to start chasing him! I thought, *I bet that was his car in the parking lot and when he gets to it, he's going to pick up his cell phone and call the police and say, "It's a GIRL up there terrorizing everybody!"* Poor guy is probably still in therapy trying to get past his phobia of women in the woods with their hands over their heads.

Haven't you ever seen something and thought for sure you knew what it was only to realize moments later that your initial perception was way off? Maybe a foreboding dark shape beside the garage at night that turns out to be a trashcan instead of a would-be intruder? Or an eerie shape coming toward you in the ocean that turns out to be the reflection of a cloud overhead instead of a Great White getting ready to bite?

Scaring an innocent, relaxed hiker in a mountain meadow or unnecessarily alerting a lifeguard because of a cloud are mild consequences compared to the damage that occurs when our view of the King of kings gets blurry—which happens all too often when our emotions run high or our circumstances seem scary. So let's endeavor to look at God really closely and really carefully—in His Word, by His Spirit, and through prayer, thereby wiping the smudge off our spiritual lenses and squelching our propensity to panic!

- **WHAT WONDERFUL CHARACTERISTIC** of God have you recently discovered after years of not seeing that "grace right in front of your face"?

- **WHAT TYPICALLY OBSCURES** your view of God, or tempts you to view Him the wrong way?

- **HOW HAS GOD** corrected your view of Him in past seasons? How might that help you in this season?

Day 60
FIGHTING FOR BREATH

Everyone who hates his brother or sister is a murderer, and you know that no murderer has eternal life residing in him. This is how we have come to know love: He laid down his life for us. We should also lay down our lives for our brothers and sisters. If anyone has this world's goods and sees a fellow believer in need but withholds compassion from him—how does God's love reside in him? 1 JOHN 3:15–17

DURING THE FIRST SUMMER of COVID-19, I was standing outside my friend Shardey's salon because social distancing parameters only allowed for one person to be inside with the stylist at any given time. So my beautiful brown-skinned daughter was in there with Shardey, happily waving at me through the window, thoroughly enjoying the air conditioning while she got her gorgeous, curly hair braided. And there I was: outside in the Tennessee heat, sweating like a sumo wrestler in a sauna on that muggy, early summer morning!

Truth be told, I was actually grateful for that hour of physical separation from Missy because my heart was shredded in the wake of yet another black man killed by unwarranted police brutality, not to mention the national outrage and division it's caused. In this case, a man in Minneapolis named George Floyd died after being arrested on the suspicion that he'd tried to use a counterfeit twenty-dollar bill to purchase cigarettes at a nearby convenience store. Following a 911 call reporting a suspect that matched Mr. Floyd's description, police officers pulled him out of his van, and one held him down on the ground, with his knee in Mr. Floyd's neck. This compromised his air supply for almost nine minutes.

Mr. Floyd's cries, "I can't breathe! I can't breathe!" got weaker and weaker while bystanders pleaded with the officer to quit choking him since he was lying on the ground moaning, obviously not resisting arrest.

I firmly believe that most folks in our police forces around the country are good and decent human beings who choose to pursue a career in civil service because they feel called to protect their fellow citizens from harm and ensure public safety. Often at the risk of their own lives. Yet at the same time, I believe there are also a few rotten apples in every institution. Because sin lies in every human heart, and by extension, in every single system human beings create. Fallen people create fallen groups of people, which creates fallen institutions. Even in so-called *good* groups of people, ones that God deems important and necessary and valuable, we will still find fallenness on full display. A badge can't make someone intrinsically good any more than ethnicity can make someone intrinsically bad. God doesn't declare us good or bad based on the group we belong to or our vocational training; it's the posture of our hearts before Him that counts. The bottom line is: every group, no matter who they are or why they exist, has unredemptive elements represented within it. And it's really, really hard when you see unredeemed, rotten behavior carried out, isn't it? Especially when it harms a person who looks a lot like your own daughter.

I needed time alone in the parking lot to weep and wail and beseech God for mercy on behalf of other moms and dads of beautiful brown children who've stopped waving back happily because they've come to the sober realization that they live in a world where they have to be wary just to stay alive. Just to breathe.

Regarding the Holocaust, Elie Wiesel wrote, "The opposite of love is not hate, it's indifference."[11] I don't have any new wisdom to share regarding how to eradicate the systemic evil of racism, but I'm committed to listen and learn and look at what's really going on. And I'm committed to *stand up*—shoulder to shoulder and hand in hand—with my friends, my daughter, and all other image-bearers for their right to breathe. Racism is real. It's the antithesis of the Gospel, which brings all ethnicities together under the banner of Christ. Yes, rottenness and racism are alive and well. But love has the power to overcome it.

- **HAVE YOU (OR** any of your loved ones) been abused, ridiculed, oppressed and/or treated unfairly because of your/their ethnicity?

- **IF SO, HOW** did you/they respond?

- **WHAT STEPS ARE** you currently taking to help put a stop to racism, bigotry, and ethnic oppression in your corner of the world? What might it look like for you to show others what being united in Christ looks like in a world of division?

Day 61

POWER NAPPING

*The L*ORD *is good, a stronghold in a day of distress; he cares for those who take refuge in him.* NAHUM 1:7

OUR LITTLE FAMILY HAS recently faced a busier-than-usual season—actually a tad too busy—for both avoidable and unavoidable reasons (despite years of therapy, saying "no" still isn't my strong suit, but my counselor has assured me that I'm showing steady signs of improvement!). However, one night when I got home from Atlanta and knew I had gobs to do before leaving again at 6:30 a.m. the next morning for a flight to Oklahoma, I felt that little nudge to pause for a moment, and—miracle of miracles!—I listened. I stopped and took the time to sit on the deck and hum worship songs while watching a storm roll in as Missy watched her favorite animated movie on her iPad, happily sprawled right beside me.

What I've discovered after being a burn-the-candle-at-both-ends kind of girl for decades is that God and others-oriented priorities can sometimes preempt the rarely attainable goal of balance. Furthermore, the length and location of whatever "respite" looks like for us isn't nearly as important as the *Who* we lean into during long seasons or short moments of soul care. If you're like me and would rate yourself as a slow learner in the subject of calendar margins (or maybe you're a single parent with one too many legitimate responsibilities who'd like to kick the next person who lectures you about carving out "me time" squarely in the shins!), may I encourage you to throw whatever breadcrumbs of time and energy you have on the calm waters of Christ's sufficiency?

Let's all pray for divine wisdom to know what to say yes to and what to say no to in light of what's actually in accordance with God's plan and purpose for our particular life. But let's also endeavor to enjoy more catnaps in the tender, restorative arms of our Creator-Redeemer when we've got too much on our plate to enjoy a complete hibernation!

- **HOW WOULD YOU** define a mini-vacation with God?

- **WHEN'S THE LAST** time you took one?

- **IN THE NEXT** week or month, what slivers of time could you dedicate to resting in the Lord?

Day 62

THE HOLINESS OF HELPLESSNESS

Immediately the father of the boy cried out,
"I do believe; help my unbelief!" MARK 9:24

———————

EIGHT MONTHS AFTER I brought Missy home from Haiti, she got sick for the first time. Up until that dreadful evening, she'd been really healthy. I mean she had some nasty parasites and stuff that we had to treat with antibiotics right after she came home and she has seasonal allergies, but other than that, she's a tough little peanut. I did my best to remain calm after noticing that her eyes were glassy and she had an elevated temperature. I got her in her favorite pajamas, gave her a dose of children's Tylenol, and encouraged her to sip Pedialyte while I sat beside her on the bed and read some of her favorite books out loud.

But after about an hour, when the thermometer showed that her temperature was rising, I could feel my heart rate going up too. I couldn't help but remember the scary stories I'd read about kids with compromised immune systems who got something as innocuous as a cold that rapidly turned into pneumonia. So I called my friend Kathleen who's a surgeon and a mom.

"Kathleen, I'm trying not to be a Nervous Nellie but Missy's temperature is almost 102 and I need you to talk me off a cliff because I'm pretty close to bundling her up and racing to the ER."

She responded with her characteristic calmness and asked me the following questions:

Is she able to drink clear liquids and has she been urinating normally? Yes.

Did her fever go down after you gave her the first dose of Tylenol? Yes.

Has she been vomiting? No.

Is she complaining of a severe headache? No.

When you depress the skin on her forearm does it immediately return to normal or does it remain indented? It went right back to normal.

Has she lost consciousness since she got sick? No. But she's limp when I pick her up to take her to the bathroom and is acting really lethargic.

Kathleen then said, "Lease, I will be *glad* to get in the car right now and meet you at the ER, but I think this is just a typical childhood virus. I know it's scary because this is the first time she's had a high fever, but I don't think this has anything to do with her HIV. High fevers are incredibly common in little kids, and as long as it's responding to Tylenol and she's drinking fluids and urinating, she's going to be fine. As a matter of fact, she'll probably be back to normal by the morning."

After Kathleen assured me that I could call her *anytime* throughout the night regardless of how late it was and reiterated her willingness to meet me at the ER, she gave me a gentle word of caution. She said, "Now Lisa, let me warn you about one thing. Sometimes high fevers cause children to have mild hallucinations and in that case, they can say crazy things. So if Missy does that, please call me immediately, but don't panic, okay?"

I wish I could tell you I heeded Dr. William's advice, but she may as well have told me not to eat the hot bread they bring out before the entrée at Italian restaurants. Because about an hour later, when I was tenderly wiping Missy's forehead with a cold washcloth and she mumbled, "I see Jebus, mama. I see Jebus," I completely freaked out. I wrapped my arms around her little shoulders and, in my best Christian-mother moment, I shouted, "Run away from Him, honey. RUN AWAY!" Because I was terrified that Missy's feverish vision of the Good Shepherd was going to be followed by a long tunnel and a bright light and if she walked toward Him, she was going to zip up to heaven right then and there! Much like that ancient daddy who was worried about his sick kid in Mark 9, God had to help with my unbelief when mine got sick too.

Now, suffice it to say that Missy made it through that terrible night, and so did I! However, something hit me in the midst of all of it: that simple confession—*I believe but help me in my unbelief*—is basically the story of my life. And if you're honest, I bet it's a familiar refrain in yours as well. But be encouraged, your admitted crisis of belief may very well usher in the biggest spiritual breakthrough of your life. Because as one of my favorite pastors and theologians, Dr. Tim Keller, says: "Helplessness, not holiness, is the first step to accessing God."[12]

- **WHAT KINDS OF** situations cause you to cry out this sort of confession to God?

- **HOW HAVE YOU** seen Him pull through for you?

- **WHAT "KATHLEEN" FIGURE** has God placed in your life to help you remain steady during wobbly seasons?

Day 63

GRADED ON A CURVE

"This is my servant; I strengthen him,
this is my chosen one; I delight in him.
I have put my Spirit on him;
he will bring justice to the nations.
He will not cry out or shout
or make his voice heard in the streets.
He will not break a bruised reed,
and he will not put out a smoldering wick;
he will faithfully bring justice." ISAIAH 42:1–3

LUKE'S NARRATIVE DESCRIBES JOHN the Baptist as Jesus' second cousin. Why? Because Johnny B's mom was Elizabeth, who was Mary's first cousin. And they weren't just relatives, they were the oldest of friends because they met before they were even born and Johnny B was apparently so excited by the encounter, he jumped up and down in Elizabeth's pregnant belly and gave her terrible indigestion (Luke 1:39–44). It may even be technically correct to say the Gospel was first legitimized when Liz took a Tums. But I digress.

Anyway, Jesus and John the Baptist surely climbed jungle gyms together when they were young and their moms were chatting over coffee, but they didn't see much of each other during their teens and twenties because John moved out to the Judean desert after being orphaned by his elderly parents—Zechariah and Elizabeth (Luke 1:80).

While Jesus was growing up in a noisy household with two loving parents and a gaggle of brothers and sisters, John came of age in the austere silence of the wilderness. While Jesus conversed with Rabbis and celebrated religious festivals, John fasted and prayed in solitude. And the older they got, the odder John seemed to get. Not only did he abstain from socializing and alcohol (dutifully following the instructions an angel gave his dad before he was born; Luke 1:5–25), but he began wearing putrid animal skins and eating bugs and honey. Then things got even weirder when John the Baptist offended the king's trashy new wife, who was formerly wed to the king's half-brother, and got thrown into the slammer (Matt. 14:1–4)!

And while he was incarcerated, the disparity between he and Jesus threatened to become an impassible divide: Now when John heard in prison what the Christ was doing, he sent a message through his disciples and asked him, "Are you the one who is to come, or should we expect someone else?" (Matt. 11:2–3).

In other words, John was asking Jesus, "Are You *really* the Messiah? I mean, good night, Cuz, here I've been slaving away in the desert without wine, women, or Netflix, and You're going to parties, hanging out with drunks at happy hour, and telling people to love those who persecute them? I don't get it."

It's understandable that John started getting suspicious if Jesus really *was* the Lamb of God like he had once declared Him to be. It makes sense that his dedication wavered. I mean he was wasting away in jail, and the circumstances at the time didn't quite look like this Messiah knew what He doing. Sure, I get the moment of unbelief. But still. Don't you think this guy should've at least been reprimanded for doubting the divinity of the Christ? Wouldn't you expect at least one of those "Oh you of little faith!" statements to fly out of Jesus' mouth right about this time? I know, me too. Thankfully for Johnny B—and for us!—our Creator-Redeemer is slow to anger and rich in compassion (Ps. 145:8). Instead of condemning His cousin for getting weary on his walk of faith, our Savior sent a very encouraging personal message regarding fulfilled prophecy, then essentially grabbed a megaphone, began a "Johnny B" cheer, and incited the crowd to do the wave in his honor:

> Jesus told them, "Go back and tell John what's going on:
> The blind see,
> The lame walk,
> Lepers are cleansed,
> The deaf hear,
> The dead are raised,
> The wretched of the earth learn that God is on their side.
> "Is this what you were expecting? Then count yourselves most blessed!"

When John's disciples left to report, Jesus started talking to the crowd about John. "What did you expect when you went out to see him in the wild? A weekend camper? Hardly. What then? A sheik in silk pajamas? Not in the wilderness, not by a long shot. What then? A prophet? That's right, a prophet! Probably the best prophet you'll ever hear. He is the prophet that Malachi announced when he wrote, 'I'm sending my prophet ahead of you, to make the road smooth for you.'" (Matt. 11:4–10 MSG)

- **HOW HAS GOD** given you a figurative high-five when you deserved a time-out?

- **IN MOMENTS OF** doubt or suspicion, how has Jesus helped you remember that He really is all that the Bible says He is?

- **HOW DOES JESUS'** demeanor toward John encourage you as you face wilderness seasons of your own?

Day 64
KNOT-FREE TANGLES

Brothers and sisters, if someone is overtaken in any wrongdoing, you who are spiritual, restore such a person with a gentle spirit, watching out for yourselves so that you also won't be tempted. Carry one another's burdens; in this way you will fulfill the law of Christ. For if anyone considers himself to be something when he is nothing, he deceives himself. GALATIANS 6:1–3

A YOUNG CHRISTIAN RECENTLY asked me, "What's the difference between 'seeing sin' in someone else's life and simply confronting it versus having a critical spirit?" I told her I thought the key distinction between *recognizing and confronting* behavior that's ungodly in someone else and *passing judgment* on others is the posture of our own hearts. Are we aware of other people's mistakes because they trust us and have confided in us, or have we appointed ourselves as the "moral police" so as to justify examining blemishes in everyone else's behavior? Because as ambassadors of Christ, part of our job description is to help *restore* prodigals into a redemptive relationship with Him (1 Cor. 5:11–12), not try to elevate ourselves by exposing other people's flaws! Though the confrontational conversation can look mighty similar in terms of the exact words exchanged, God knows our real motive—either we are trying to tear someone down for the sake of feeling better about ourselves, or we are trying to build another person up for the sake of their good.

One of the most often quoted passages from the Bible regarding confronting someone in sin is:

> "If your brother sins against you, go tell him his fault, between you and him alone. If he listens to you, you have won your brother. But if he won't listen, take one or two others with you, so that by the testimony of two or three witnesses every fact may be established. If he doesn't pay attention to them, tell the church. If he doesn't pay attention even to the church, let him be like a Gentile and a tax collector to you." (Matt. 18:15–17)

Which at first pass sounds pretty punitive. Unless we pause long enough to remember how Jesus actually dealt with tax collectors and Gentiles in the Gospels: He *loved* them! Therefore, while some Christians and communities of faith use the above passage to justify disciplinary consequences for those who've stepped over a whopper of a line, like having an extramarital affair or slandering another believer (and the New Testament does include teaching and templates for how believers should be held accountable by church leadership), I think it behooves us to focus on the restorative grace implied by Jesus in the above passage. Of course, we need parameters in place to help identify, prevent, and rectify wanton sinful behavior in our communities of faith, but perhaps even more importantly we must remember Jesus' aim is to *restore* wayward souls back to the way of life, not beat "the bad" out of them!

I've been confronted twice lately by other Christians; one came from a red-faced stranger who was furious with me for wearing knee-high leather boots and a skirt (which came to well below my knees) to her church. She actually called me a "Jezebel" and said God would not bless me unless I started dressing more appropriately. Thank goodness I hadn't ridden my motorcycle to her house of worship because then I would've been clad in leather pants, and she likely would've tried to have me stoned! The second confrontation came from a good friend, who tenderly pointed out my pride in a specific situation she'd been involved in. That confrontation included tears—*hers*—because my friend was much more concerned about my restoration than about being right. The name-calling lady had no redemptive affect. But my friend's compassionate correction turned me back toward the forgiving arms of our heavenly Father in genuine repentance. And that right there is the difference.

As Christ followers, we've got to recognize that God alone has the perfect combination of holiness and mercy to stand in judgment of the human heart. Plus, we have to remember the only One worthy of condemning us chose instead to pay for our wrongdoing Himself and then pardon us! Then, in light of our own sinner-saved-by-grace stories—and only when the Holy Spirit impresses us to address someone else's error—we'll do so with honesty, compassion, and humility. The bottom line is, if you're feeling giddy about catching someone else red-handed and you have several "confrontation speech" options saved on your laptop, you probably ought to keep your mouth shut for now.

- **WHAT'S THE MOST** compassionate correction you've received lately?

- **DID IT HELP** you move toward God in repentance or away from Him—and the "confronter"—in resentment? Why?

- **HOW MIGHT GOD** be leading you to lovingly correct someone dear to you in this season of life, with a genuine aim of restoration and not condemnation? Or, on the flip side, how might God be leading you to lovingly receive correction that could restore you to the way of life?

Day 65

ERADICATING LOCUSTS EVERYWHERE

I will repay you for the years
that the swarming locust ate,
the young locust, the destroying locust,
and the devouring locust—
my great army that I sent against you.
You will have plenty to eat and be satisfied.
You will praise the name of the LORD your God,
who has dealt wondrously with you.
My people will never again be put to shame.
You will know that I am present in Israel
and that I am the LORD your God,
and there is no other.
My people will never again be put to shame. JOEL 2:25–27

———————

WHILE TROTTING DOWN AN almost deserted Florida beach toward our hotel on a recent rainy day, it occurred to me that Missy and I were on our first *real* vacation. We've been on scores of work trips and mission trips and several vacations with friends and family members, but it was the very first time just the two of us had some uninterrupted down time away from home that wasn't associated with my work and/or didn't include someone else. And while the weather remained uncooperative the entire three days my little girl and I got to spend alone at the beach (we were forced inside by thunderstorms and had to cocoon ourselves in multiple layers for warmth during the rare hours when the sun did shine), we still had a fantastic time!

We got so tickled while schlepping our stuff back to the hotel room from the beach during yet another monsoon, that we collapsed deep into the wet sand in a full-on giggle fit! We spent one long rainy afternoon sprawled contentedly on the too-soft hotel bed: she shared her Cheetos with me until all twenty of our fingers were stained bright orange, and I shared every single thing I knew about her first mama, Marie (who died of undiagnosed AIDS when Missy was just a baby), until Missy ran out of questions.

Lying there, the lovely realization hit me that I have a lifetime—or at least until Jesus returns or she gets her driver's license—of rainy days, giggle-fits, and talk-fests to share with my daughter. Which caused me to smile inwardly and whisper "Thank You" to God for restoring unto me several decades of life that I'd unwittingly served up to locusts on a silver platter. And I made a mental promise not to let fear or foolish choices ever again keep me, much less my miracle of a daughter, from the abundant life God graciously planned and generously provided for us.

Whether the figurative weather in my future is sunny or stormy, from this day forward I aim to spend it swimming in the cool, clean current of God's will instead of flailing about miserably in the muddy trickle of my own!

- **HOW RESOLVED ARE** you not to repeat the mistakes of your past?

- **WHAT USUALLY TEMPTS** you to keep your perspective focused on the things that "locusts have eaten" as opposed to the gracious gifts God has given you?

- **WHAT KIND OF** "locust damage" has God restored in your life lately?

Day 66

THE BEST BENADRYL FOR ITCHY EARS

I solemnly charge you before God and Christ Jesus, who is going to judge the living and the dead, and because of his appearing and his kingdom: Preach the word; be ready in season and out of season; correct, rebuke, and encourage with great patience and teaching. For the time will come when people will not tolerate sound doctrine, but according to their own desires, will multiply teachers for themselves because they have an itch to hear what they want to hear. They will turn away from hearing the truth and will turn aside to myths. But as for you, exercise self-control in everything, endure hardship, do the work of an evangelist, fulfill your ministry. 2 TIMOTHY 4:1–5

OUR MODERN AGE IS intrigued by the concept of some kind of knowable God. But the Bible also reveals the supremacy of our Savior Jesus Christ—that a relationship with Him is the *only* way to truly know God or be rightly reconciled to Him (John 14:6). And that exclusivity, which is the very cornerstone of Christian orthodoxy, is what fosters the indignant resistance that seems to be rising in the world around us. Humanity has always longed for the divine; we just don't want the divine to give us directives.

It'd be easier if Scripture had simply referred to Jesus as a life-coach instead of the Lord of all lords (1 Tim. 6:15; Rev. 17:14; 19:16), wouldn't it? I mean no one could accuse a cover-to-cover, Bible-believing Christian of being narrow-minded or judgmental or legalistic then, right? Fortunately, we don't have the authority, much less the power, to mitigate the promises and parameters God established for the redemption of mankind. And if we did have the capacity to widen the Gospel gate He designed, we'd do irreparable damage. Because when people step outside of the boundaries our Creator Redeemer *established for all of our good,* they don't just walk away from the future and hope He's planned for us as His image-bearers, they actually forfeit their freedom.

Sin is an attractive recruiter at first, with an alluring sales pitch about how you can enjoy a life without limits. But it soon morphs into an abusive and increasingly restrictive master, unwilling to loosen the shackles that keep its victims captive. We've all experienced it at some point—that thing we once thought would give us freedom eventually put us in chains.

So stay the course, dear ones. Don't turn aside toward myths or be afraid of the truth. Resist the post-Christian cultural trendiness of only adhering to inspirational Bible passages that fit your personality type and editing out the ones that step on our all-too-human toes. The holy and holistic Word of God is a lamp unto our feet and a light unto our paths (Ps. 119:105) and without it, we're bound to ram our heads into so many walls that we'll lose the ability to think straight! I'm pretty sure he'd be dismissed as a hatemonger if he were alive today, but I still think John the apostle says it really well in his valediction:

> Both the Spirit and the bride say, "Come!" Let anyone who hears, say, "Come!" Let the one who is thirsty come. Let the one who desires take the water of life freely. I testify to everyone who hears the words of the prophecy of this book: If anyone adds to them, God will add to him the plagues that are written in this book. And if anyone takes away from the words of the book of this prophecy, God will take away his share of the tree of life and the holy city, which are written about in this book. He who testifies about these things says, "Yes, I am coming soon." Amen! Come, Lord Jesus! The grace of the Lord Jesus be with everyone. Amen. (Rev. 22:17–21)

- **WHAT BIBLE PASSAGE** seems to be the brightest light for the pathway you're on this season?

- **WHAT SPECIFIC SORT** of sin struggle tends to promise you freedom while luring you back into chains?

- **WHAT PLACES IN** Scripture step on your toes? Why do you think that is actually a good thing in the end?

Day 67

A GOD WHO STOOPS

For we do not have a high priest who is unable to sympathize with our weaknesses, but one who has been tempted in every way as we are, yet without sin. HEBREWS 4:15

THE SINGLE MOST EMBARRASSING moment of my childhood—and it ranks up there as one of the most embarrassing moments of my life—took place in church. But before I confess it, I'd like to share two qualifications.

The first is that the church I began attending while I was still in utero and remained an upstanding member of until I graduated from college was a large, conservative Baptist assembly in Central Florida. Our worship services took place in a big pink stucco building that also hosted monthly meetings of the Daughters of the American Revolution. In short, it was a rather dignified place to meet on Sundays and Wednesday nights, where hymnals were used and hands were definitely *not* raised!

The second qualification is that my mom is a Southern belle. She's gracious and appropriate and it was her great hope to pass those characteristics on to my sister, Theresa, and me. Which is why books on etiquette were required reading when I was growing up and why we spent many an afternoon walking down the hallway in our house toward a large mirror with those same thick books balanced on our heads to improve our posture. Mom did not approve of sloth, bad penmanship, using the salad fork for entrees, or any mention of bodily functions. She actually told us on several occasions that "breaking wind" anywhere except in the restroom by one's self was unacceptable because God gave us the ability to control our bodies and furthermore human "wind" consisted of methane five gas, which can be dangerous if inhaled in large quantities.

Now in light of our church's relatively formal atmosphere and my mother's disdain for certain bodily functions, you've probably already guessed where this story is heading.

It was a Sunday night service in the summer and I was six years old. I don't remember all of the details from that fateful evening, only a few. I remember it was an especially long and hot service. Which is probably why Mom motioned that I could lie down on the pew and put my head in her lap. Unfortunately, at the exact moment I scooted down to Mom's end of the pew, our pastor—Brother Freddie—paused, so when I accidentally broke wind, it was essentially the toot heard round the world. It echoed off the baby blue carpet and stained glassed windows with a mortifying amount of amplification . . . like someone had stepped on a massive whoopee cushion.

What happened immediately after my colossal faux pas is all a blur; however, I can remember *exactly* what happened when the service was over. Brother Freddie walked to his usual spot at the back of the church so that he could greet everyone as they filed out of the sanctuary. I lolly gagged toward the end of the line and tried to make myself as small as possible—hoping to sneak past him because I just *knew* he was going to lecture me about the egregiousness of my windy sin. But he noticed me trying to slink past and put out his hand to stop me.

Then that wonderful, kind man stooped down to my six-year-old level so that we could be eye to eye. He grinned and said something along the lines of, "That's the most entertained I've been in church in a long time." And he hugged me. Instead of lecturing me, that tender shepherd leaned down and loved on me.

How much more amazing is it that the King of all kings condescended from His throne in glory to make grace accessible to sinners like us? Jesus set down his royal scepter and picked up a wet towel to wash our feet. Our divine Shepherd stoops so that you and I don't have to remain forever red-faced with shame over our flaws. Hallelujah, what a Savior!

- **HOW HAVE YOU** experienced God's tenderness recently?

- **WHAT SORTS OF** flaws do you try to hide from God?

- **IN WHAT WAYS** has Jesus made it possible for you to never have to slink away from God's presence again?

Day 68
WHO'S GOT YOUR BACK?

When he entered Capernaum again after some days, it was reported that he was at home. So many people gathered together that there was no more room, not even in the doorway, and he was speaking the word to them. They came to him bringing a paralytic, carried by four of them. Since they were not able to bring him to Jesus because of the crowd, they removed the roof above him, and after digging through it, they lowered the mat on which the paralytic was lying. Seeing their faith, Jesus told the paralytic, "Son, your sins are forgiven." MARK 2:1–5

— , · — —

I LOVE TUESDAY MORNINGS because that's when I get to hang out with a group of beautifully authentic women (from a wide range of church and unchurched backgrounds) in an informal home Bible study we started about twelve years ago. And I'm hoping we get to hang for at least another twenty-five years of Tuesdays because Belle's living room houses such a deep well of true friendship, hard-knocks-kind-of-shared-wisdom, gentle correction, fierce loyalty, and raucous laughter—especially when the fire alarm goes off repeatedly during a lovely and intimate prayer time!

We've shared so much life together—we've limped through heartbreaking divorces, grieved the deaths of loved ones, danced at weddings, welcomed each other's adopted children home at the airport, gotten baptized in the Jordan River, ridden roller coasters at Dollywood, been each other's shoulders to cry on, and have at some point pretty much all been the one on the mat who desperately needed to be carried to the roof and lowered to Jesus. The rapture and rupture of real life we've experienced together has proven that a thriving community of Christ-followers isn't about having it all together, much less looking alike or thinking alike or even worshiping alike.

Quite frankly, I think the drive to look exactly like everyone else more often than not becomes a barrier to true communal intimacy. Because a lack of diversity effectively narrows the circle of who's welcome and what's appropriate until those inside the proverbial circle find themselves nervously balancing on one foot to keep from getting booted to the curb themselves.

Instead, the divine gift of community is about wrapping all of our God-given uniqueness around the supremely authoritative axis of our Creator Redeemer and the life-giving promises in His Word, which then frees us to forge a miraculously miscellaneous, Jesus-shaped family of faith.

- **IF THAT STRIKES** a chord with you, how about calling or texting the people you trust to help lug your mat to the Lord and liberally sloshing some friendship-fertilizing gratitude on them?

- **IF YOU DON'T** have friends who will carry you to Jesus, how can you make some in this season of your life?

- **WHO IN YOUR** life might need you to carry them on the mat to Jesus?

Day 69

OUR EMPATHETIC HERO

Therefore, he had to be like his brothers and sisters in every way, so that he could become a merciful and faithful high priest in matters pertaining to God, to make atonement for the sins of the people. For since he himself has suffered when he was tempted, he is able to help those who are tempted. HEBREWS 2:17–18

―――――――――――

JESUS WAS DESPERATE IN the garden of Gethsemane. He surely had the stooped shoulders and bloodshot eyes of a man in agony. In Matthew's account of what took place during those dark hours, it says Jesus was so troubled He told the disciples: *My heart is full of sorrow, to the point of death* (Matt. 26:38a NCV) and in Dr. Luke's version, he adds the medical note that the Messiah was under such extreme stress: *His sweat was like drops of blood falling to the ground* (Luke 22:44b NCV).

Contrary to some sermons I've heard over the years, Jesus didn't square His shoulders and face the cross with unblinking fortitude. He wasn't some stoic martyr; He experienced distress. Not because our Savior was afraid to die, but because He dreaded being separated from His Father and receiving God's wrath. Yet He endured that unimaginable ache alone. Even mouthy, well-intentioned Peter, who'd vowed to stick to Jesus like Velcro, fell asleep while the Messiah mourned under those gnarled olive trees.

Our Savior was bereft of companionship. No one dropped by with a pint of chicken soup. No one wrote Him a note expressing their condolences. Every single person abandoned Him during His time of deepest need.

Which is why the author of Hebrews was able to galvanize a bunch of exhausted, New Testament believers who were limping in their walk of faith with the good news that Jesus had already blazed the trail they were stumbling on. Because Jesus didn't skip to the front of the pain line. Instead He chose to be an empathetic Hero—sharing perfectly in the frailty and loneliness of our humanity.

C. S. Lewis eloquently describes this miracle of divine empathy: "But supposing God became a man—suppose our human nature which can suffer and die was amalgamated with God's nature in one person—then that person could help us. . . . That is the sense in which He pays our debt, and suffers for us what He Himself need not suffer at all."[13] May our hearts be bent in gratitude over the sacrificial and substitutional death our Redeemer chose so that we could call the Friday before Easter "good."

- **POET ELLA WHEELER** Wilcox wrote, "Laugh, and the world laughs with you; weep, and you weep alone," but the Bible says that God stores our tears in a bottle (Ps. 56:8). How does it make you feel that sorrow and isolation don't have to be joined at the hip? That God wants to be near you when you're in distress?

- **HAVE YOU EVER** leaned against God's chest when your own was heaving with grief?

- **HOW DOES JESUS'** experience in Gethsemane empower you in your darkest moments?

Day 70
TRUSTING GOD ENOUGH TO BE TRANSIENT

As they were traveling on the road someone said to him, "I will follow you wherever you go." Jesus told him, "Foxes have dens, and birds of the sky have nests, but the Son of Man has no place to lay his head." Then he said to another, "Follow me." "Lord," he said, "first let me go bury my father." But he told him, "Let the dead bury their own dead, but you go and spread the news of the kingdom of God." Another said, "I will follow you, Lord, but first let me go and say good-bye to those at my house." But Jesus said to him, "No one who puts his hand to the plow and looks back is fit for the kingdom of God." LUKE 9:57–62

THEOLOGIANS CONCUR THAT ONE of the most comprehensive blessings God the Father made to a human being is the one He made to Abraham: "Abe, I'm going to make you the father of many nations. And not only am I going to bless you but I'm going to curse those who don't bless you" (Gen. 12:1–3). That'd be sort of like God giving us high metabolisms and hair that's not chemically dependent AND giving all of the hateful people in our lives hives! Plus, God told Abe there was only one thing he had to do to receive this awesome, comprehensive, 360-degree whopper of a divine blessing—just one itty, bitty caveat: he had to leave Ur.

That's right, Abe had to walk away from the place he and his family called home. The town where he'd effectively been voted mayor. Where everybody waved when he drove down Main Street to the feed store. Where Sarah hosted a huge quilting club in their living room. Where their kids played on Little League baseball teams and co-captained the cheerleading travel team. They had to release their grip on everything comfortable in order to accept God's promises. And this isn't the only instance God asked something difficult of Abraham. The biblical theme connecting relinquishment and redemption shows up again in Abraham's story when he gets to witness God's miraculous provision of a sacrificial ram, but only after he was willing to lay down what was most precious to him:

> Abraham looked up and saw a ram caught in the thicket by its horns. So Abraham went and took the ram and offered it as a burnt

offering in place of his son. And Abraham named that place The LORD Will Provide, so today it is said, "It will be provided on the LORD's mountain." Then the angel of the LORD called to Abraham a second time from heaven and said, "By myself I have sworn," this is the LORD's declaration: "Because you have done this thing and have not withheld your only son, I will indeed bless you and make your offspring as numerous as the stars of the sky and the sand on the seashore. Your offspring will possess the city gates of their enemies. And all the nations of the earth will be blessed by your offspring because you have obeyed my command." (Gen. 22:13–18)

We all want God's blessing, don't we? Yet we aren't necessarily willing to *leave* where we've grown comfortable and *lay down* that which is most precious to us. Perhaps it's time to begin practicing the art of letting go.

- **DID THE UNCERTAINTY** and loss caused by COVID-19 help loosen your grip on comfort?

- **DO YOU THINK** you'd now be willing to leave the place and people you call home in order to please God and receive a bigger blessing if He asked you?

- **WHAT MIGHT GOD** be calling you to leave or lay down in this season, specifically?

Day 71

THE CLEANSING ACT OF CONFESSION

*The one who conceals his sins will not prosper, but whoever confesses
and renounces them will find mercy.* PROVERBS 28:13

I WASN'T WHAT YOU'D describe as an actively disobedient kid. I mean if my parents specifically told me *not* to do something, I typically complied. However, if my parents neglected to forbid me to do something, well then it was fair game.

Like when they neglected to tell me that it wasn't a good idea to leave a nice girl's eighth grade slumber party in the middle of the night with a wild girl who thought she knew a shortcut to the McDonald's that was twelve miles away by car. At the time it sounded logical—even compassionate—to traipse across town at two o'clock in the morning so as to bring back nourishment for our peers. Good night, if those survival reality television shows were popular in the late '70s, we probably would've been *lauded* for our brave ingenuity instead of being firmly reprimanded by two policemen when we come limping back to the soiree around noon, many hours after our empty sleeping bags were discovered.

After enduring the emotive sobs and entreaties of said good girl (who felt very betrayed that we didn't invite her to accompany us on the ill-fated adventure), the frosty disapproval of her parents, and a second, even harsher reprimand from my mom and stepdad on the way home, I decided it would be best not to disclose the nasty cut on the bottom of my right foot that was a result of stepping on a broken bottle while wearing flip flops on the trek.

When the cut began to throb that night, I held my foot over the bathtub, doused it with rubbing alcohol, then wrapped it in an Ace bandage and made a mental note to wear sturdier footwear if I ever went on another nighttime excursion. When it hurt too badly to stand on the next morning, I told mom I thought I was coming down with the flu—a white lie she swallowed whole after taking my temperature and finding it to be unusually high.

It wasn't until later that day, when mom asked if there was anything I had omitted from the slumber-party-disappearance story that I confessed everything. Which is when she lifted up the sheet and saw the angry red streaks—signs of a serious infection—running up and down my leg. Naturally, she bundled me into the Buick and raced to the hospital. Which is where a white-headed doctor with protruding Albert-Einstein-ish eyebrows told me kindly but firmly, "This is going to hurt something awful, honey, but we don't have time for you to get numb if we're going to save your foot!" You can understand why I don't remember much else after seeing the flash of his scalpel and watching Mom slump into a plastic chair to keep from fainting.

I knew from the moment I stepped on that broken bottle and it sliced my instep that it was a nasty cut, but I assumed it was nothing a little rubbing alcohol couldn't cure. I was much more concerned about whether it would keep me from competing in the track meet our team had scheduled later that week. Or whether I would get grounded if Mom found out about the injury. And the concern that weighed *most* heavily on my adolescent mind was whether I'd end up losing phone privileges, which would surely render me a thirteen-year-old pariah. My life would never go on! It never occurred to me that sepsis could cause me to lose my foot or, as the doctor soberly told my mom afterwards, possibly even my life. Yet with just one act of confession, my foot was saved, the lines of communication were opened back up with my mom, and my life, did, in fact, go on!

- **WHAT SEEMINGLY MINOR** unconfessed sins turned into serious injuries that caused you to limp for a season in your walk of faith?

- **CAN YOU REMEMBER** any times in your life where God showed you the freeing and saving power of confession? How does it feel when you "open back up" the lines of communication with Him?

- **DO YOU TEND** to confess right after a transgression now, or do you still tend to wait and hide it, hoping the wound will just heal itself?

Day 72
WE CAN DO BETTER THAN BITTER

Then God said, "Let us make man in our image, according to our likeness. They will rule the fish of the sea, the birds of the sky, the livestock, the whole earth, and the creatures that crawl on the earth." So God created man in his own image; he created him in the image of God; he created them male and female. GENESIS 1:26–27

"IN HIS OWN IMAGE." In Latin, the term that gets at this biblical principle is *Imago Dei.* And it simply means that human beings were created with inherent dignity, according to God's likeness. That's a huge thing—we weren't created in the image of inanimate objects, but in the image of *God Himself.* Which means we weren't made to be marginalized and missed and victimized and violated, which is at the root of much of the angry "we're not going to take it lying down anymore" narrative so prevalent now in modern culture. People are just flat sick and tired of putting up with abuse. Be it personal abuse like sexual molestation and discrimination or systemic abuse like racism and misogyny.

Now, I am *all about* the restoration of human value and dignity. I was sexually molested for years as a child, and raped in college, and have stories for days about being oppressed, humiliated, and undervalued by people with small minds and bad theology. My daughter Missy was orphaned in Haiti after her first mama died of AIDS, unwittingly infecting her with HIV, and she's been the victim of many racist slurs and even assaults (a couple of which I've already shared with you right here in this book!). So believe me, we've had our fair share of shame, bigotry, and marginalization.

Yet, I think some people in the community of faith have passed right by the restoration God has made available for us in their quest for *revenge*—and as we all know, restoration and revenge are two very, very different paths to take in life. The kind of value and empowerment we can absolutely derive from Scripture and being enraged are not synonymous. God's Spirit empowers us to share the living hope of Jesus Christ with a world that is desperately hungry for redemption. But an embittered, wounded spirit is what drives the kind of furious, less-than-productive diatribe we're seeing some people hurl nowadays under the banner of renewal or freedom.

I read an article recently that was written by a lovely woman I used to learn from and teach alongside. In this article she explained how being deeply hurt and offended by other Christians had compelled her to spend several years deconstructing Scripture and she now believes the Bible is something that can't be read with any certainty and faith in Jesus is not the only way by which sinners can be restored to a holy God. Actually, I don't think she used the word *sinner* because she also made it clear she doesn't believe in that kind of archaic terminology anymore, much less a theology that includes the concept of repentance.

Now, my point here isn't to throw anyone under the bus. Frankly, these kind of "deconversion" stories break my heart. My point is that the mass exodus of so many dear, wounded deserters should jar the rest of us into diving deeper into God's Word so that our experience and understanding and cognizance of His redemptive nature will resound clearer and louder and more compelling than their heartbreaking and heretical deconstruction narratives. Their wounds are real. Which should force those of us still under the banner of Christian faith to ask *why*, to fix what went wrong to the best of our ability, and to create a better, healthier narrative. When it comes to sheep who were harmed by hypocrites and liars, the answer isn't throwing all the sheep out of the fold to fend for themselves. The answer is to handle the hypocrites according to the Word of God (which tells us how to deal with wolves!) and draw even closer to the Good Shepherd and His Words—to the only One who can speak to us with the kind of power that can restore and heal!

I believe anyone who takes the time to get familiar with the overarching story of Scripture will come to the realization that God has always been in the business of reducing human suffering, restoring human dignity, and repairing the intimacy that was broken between us and Him a long, long time ago.

- **HAVE YOU EVER** felt marginalized in the context of Christianity?

- **IF SO, HOW** did it make you feel?

- **HOW HAS JESUS** helped you stay true to the faith, remain in His Word, and heal from past wounds?

Day 73

WHO'S YOUR DADDY?

How blessed is God! And what a blessing he is! He's the Father of our Master, Jesus Christ, and takes us to the high places of blessing in him. Long before he laid down earth's foundations, he had us in mind, had settled on us as the focus of his love, to be made whole and holy by his love. Long, long ago he decided to adopt us into his family through Jesus Christ. (What pleasure he took in planning this!) He wanted us to enter into the celebration of his lavish gift-giving by the hand of his beloved Son. EPHESIANS 1:3–6 MSG

A FEW YEARS AGO, when I was waiting for Missy in the school pick-up line, I became concerned she'd gotten sick during the day because she was standing in line with her head down and a very uncharacteristic forlorn expression on her face. As soon the school-crossing-guard/gestapo allowed her to climb into the backseat of our car, I asked how she was feeling while edging toward a parking space so that I could jump out of the car and check her forehead to see if she was running a fever.

She confided that she wasn't sick. She was sad because her friend George had asked, "Who's your daddy?" during math class. Now my guess is that her classmate's question was completely innocent, and he was probably just pre-occupied with which adults "belonged" to which child in light of the fact that Parent's Day was fast approaching at their school. And since George had only seen Missy walking down the hall while holding hands with me—a middle-aged pale lady—he simply wanted to be sure he recognized Missy's daddy when the time came. However, based on Missy's sagging shoulders, his innocuous query had unwittingly pierced her heart the way broken glass would a bare foot.

When I asked her how she answered his question, she soberly responded, "I told him I don't have a daddy." Suffice it to say I thought my heart was going to split in half. In the silent seconds that followed, I asked God for wisdom in how to comfort my little girl. Then I drove to a nearby park and took her for a walk down to the duck pond and found a comfortable place to sit under a tree. After I played with her hair for a little while—which always seems to soothe her—I said, "Honey, you actually do have a Daddy and His name is Daddy God.

He knew you before you were born and He loves you more than all the stars in the sky."

She thought about that for a while before asking earnestly, "Mommy, if God is my Daddy, how come He doesn't drive me to school or teach me to play soccer or make me pancakes like George's daddy?" To which I replied, "Well sweetie, Daddy God is invisible, so we can't see Him the way we can see human daddies with skin on. And even though Daddy God doesn't drive a car, coach soccer, or make pancakes, He did create the whole, wide world and He is always with you and He will never, ever leave you or stop loving you."

That first precious conversation Missy and I had about her unconditionally loving Daddy God led to a series of conversations about Him that have continued to this day. And while I had the privilege of two "skin daddies" (my dear Dad Harper and stepfather, John Angel), it didn't take me long to realize that the immutable affection and permanent presence of a heavenly Father were foundational truths I needed to be reminded of myself!

- **WOULD YOU DESCRIBE** your relationship with Father God to be more secure or insecure?

- **WHEN'S THE LAST** time (if ever) you've figuratively crawled into His lap and lingered in His embrace?

- **AS YOU LOOK** back on your life, how has God loved you like a Father?

Day 74

SOGGY SHOES

Then Joshua set up in Gilgal the twelve stones they had taken from the Jordan, and he said to the Israelites, "In the future, when your children ask their fathers, 'What is the meaning of these stones?' you should tell your children, 'Israel crossed the Jordan on dry ground.' For the LORD your God dried up the water of the Jordan before you until you had crossed over, just as the LORD your God did to the Red Sea, which he dried up before us until we had crossed over. This is so that all the peoples of the earth may know that the LORD's hand is strong, and so that you may always fear the LORD your God." JOSHUA 4:20–24

BRAVERY IS NOT SIMPLY an attitude, it's an action. For Christ-followers, bravery is putting feet to our faith even if that means walking uphill, in the rain, in roller-skates. Sometimes bravery means choosing to take the first step even though we're secretly shaking in our boots. It means trusting God more than we fear failure, abandonment, disapproval, or even death. And it's not a tribal mentality either, it's a singular decision of faith. Frankly, sometimes what the world calls "brave" is actually just a pack of frightened folks running like lemmings in the same direction.

One of my favorite stories of bravery is found in Joshua chapter 3 when our spiritual ancestors, the Israelites, make it to the finish line of their forty-year trek to the Promised Land. All that stands between them and their inheritance is the Jordan River. However, since it's at flood stage and the water is much higher (likely overflowing, actually) and rougher than usual, it probably looked nearly as impossible to cross as the Red Sea had at the beginning of their liberation adventure all those years before.

Yet instead of supernaturally paving a path through the water without asking them to lift a finger to help like He did at the Red Sea (see Exod. 14:13–14, 21–22), God now tells His people that this time they're going to have to *participate* in the miracle instead of simply observing it:

> The LORD spoke to Joshua: "Today I will begin to exalt you in the sight of all Israel, so they will know that I will be with you just as I was with Moses. Command the priests carrying the ark of

the covenant: When you reach the edge of the water, stand in the Jordan." . . . Now the Jordan overflows its banks throughout the harvest season. But as soon as the priests carrying the ark reached the Jordan, their feet touched the water at its edge and the water flowing downstream stood still, rising up in a mass that extended as far as Adam, a city next to Zarethan. The water flowing downstream into the Sea of the Arabah—the Dead Sea—was completely cut off, and the people crossed opposite Jericho. The priests carrying the ark of the LORD's covenant stood firmly on dry ground in the middle of the Jordan, while all Israel crossed on dry ground until the entire nation had finished crossing the Jordan. (Josh. 3:7–8, 15–17)

Here's the deal, y'all. God's people hadn't learned to recognize His voice yet when they encountered the Red Sea. They'd just *started* their walk of faith . . . they weren't even out of spiritual diapers. But when they got to the edge of the Jordan River, they'd experienced four long decades of Jehovah's presence, protection, and provision. The Creator of the Universe actually condescended to reveal Himself to them *tangibly*—as a cloud by day and a pillar of fire by night (Exod. 13:21–22)—for goodness sakes! They should've been more than ready to step up and get their hands dirty, or *feet wet*, as it were. It was time to *practice* all that preaching they'd heard from Big Moe!

- **HOW ABOUT YOU?** What new territory has God been prompting you to step bravely into?

- **LET'S SAY YOU** are facing something new that looks a little familiar— perhaps a struggle you've endured before that is rearing its ugly head. What might you miss out on if you don't ask God for fresh direction, but simply coast on the way He led you last time?

- **IN THIS PASSAGE,** the people of God are braving the waters together. In this season of your life, what community is walking with you through the waters?

Day 75
THE LANGUAGE OF THE DIVINE

This is the confidence we have before him: If we ask anything
according to his will, he hears us. 1 JOHN 5:14

THE SINGLE MOST DIFFICULT thing Missy and I dealt with during the first few months we got to live under the same roof as mother and daughter wasn't the frequent trips to the hospital or learning how and remembering to dispense her twice-daily dose of three different medications. It wasn't even my futile, scalp-torturing attempts to learn how to micro-braid her gorgeous Haitian hair. The most difficult, sometimes gut-wrenching, aspect of our first nose-to-nose season was learning to communicate.

Since we'd managed to *sort of* understand each other with a few common words of Creole and English coupled with facial expressions and charades throughout my many visits to Haiti during the adoption process, I wasn't fully prepared for the frustration and heartache that would result from our communication gap once I finally got to bring her home to Tennessee.

The first night she fell asleep pretty quickly, obviously exhausted after the long trip from Port-au-Prince to Tennessee. But the next night—after I'd gotten her changed into her pajamas, bundled into her toddler bed, and began singing a lullaby to help her go to sleep—Missy got very upset. I picked her up and did everything our adoption transition counselor and social worker had advised me to do when she showed signs of anxiety in order to demonstrate to her that she was safe and secure. But my actions only seemed to make things worse.

Finally, after more than an hour of her growing increasingly agitated and me vainly trying to soothe her, I went and got the Creole dictionary from the bookshelf and attempted to ask her if she was in pain. The second I began trying to articulate that foreign phrase her head snapped toward me, her brown eyes focused on mine with laser-like intensity and she began talking as fast as she could. A torrent of unfamiliar words poured from her mouth like water from a breach in a dam. After a minute or two, when she could tell by my expression that I didn't understand, she put both of her baby brown hands on the side of my face and began to speak very intently, with even more passion and volume.

Eventually I replied in English, "I'm so sorry baby, I don't understand what you're saying." At which point she dropped her hands to her side, looked away from me with hopeless resignation, and began to sob uncontrollably. All I could do was repeat one of the few Creole phrases I'd memorized, "Mwen regret sa. Mwen regret sa. Mwen regret sa." *I'm sorry. I'm sorry. I'm sorry.*

My little girl cried herself to sleep on her second night at home and when her breathing finally settled into the rhythm of slumber I walked out into the living room, sank into the couch, and cried until I didn't have any tears left either. It felt like my precious daughter—whom I'd longed for since I was a young woman and fought for through an arduous two-year adoption journey—had tried to give me her heart and it slipped through my hands.

Recently an acquaintance told me she'd like to have an intimate relationship with God, but she'd found reading the Bible boring and she wasn't really "into" prayer. I couldn't help thinking, *You're letting Living Hope slip right through your hands.* Reading the Bible and prayer are not religious chores to dutifully complete or conspicuously avoid; they are the language of the divine through which the God of the Universe graciously allows us to commune with Him. Even more so than allowing us to communicate with Him, our heavenly Father deeply *wants* us to, a million more times than I wanted to communicate with Missy that night.

It may be awkward at first, and it may take time, but I can pretty much guarantee that like Missy and me, communication will soon start flowing back and forth between you and God when you open your heart up to it!

- **DO YOU READ** the Bible and pray more out of duty or desire?

- **HAVE YOU EVER** considered just how much God wants to commune with you? How does it change things to know that He not only lets you communicate with Him, but He wants you to?

- **WHEN HAVE YOU** felt like your attempts to talk to God just weren't getting through? How did God eventually meet you in that season?

Day 76
FINAL JEOPARDY

Jesus went out with his disciples to the villages of Caesarea Philippi. And on the road he asked his disciples, "Who do people say that I am?" They answered him, "John the Baptist; others, Elijah; still others, one of the prophets." "But you," he asked them, "who do you say that I am?" Peter answered him, "<u>You are the Messiah</u>." MARK 8:27–30, EMPHASIS MINE

ONE NIGHT A FEW weeks ago Missy quietly watched me pack the carry-on suitcase lying open on the bed for a few minutes. Then she looked at me pointedly and asked, "How long are you going to be gone, Mom?" I replied, "After I take you to school in the morning, I'm flying to Dallas for a women's event. But it's only for one night and I'll be back home the next day in time to pick you up from school." She considered my reply for a few seconds then looked up with a gleam in her eyes and an impish expression on her face and declared proudly, "You're going to talk about Jesus and God and ME!" My little girl has been around me long enough to know *exactly* what I talk about whenever I have the undeserved privilege of a microphone . . . she has supreme confidence in knowing who I am and how I'm wired!

Supreme confidence.

That's what we see in Peter's confession. There's no hesitation. No hemming and hawing. He doesn't beat around the bush. There's no ifs, ands, or buts about it. *You are the Messiah, Jesus.* Period. End of story.

Jesus had been called several names up to this point in the Gospel according to Mark. At the very beginning Mark called Him "the Son of God" (1:1). Demons referred to Him as "the Holy One of God" (1:24), "the Son of God" (3:11), and "Son of the Most High God" (5:7). And while all those monikers are accurate, they somehow miss the mark (no pun intended). They have the same precise yet impersonal ring as when Missy accidentally called me "Lisa" the other day instead of "Mom." Those names adequately describe "Who" Jesus is in relation to God the Father, but they don't begin to describe "Who" He is in relation to sinners like us. Peter's answer is the only one that answers Jesus' question perfectly:

You are THE CHRIST. The Anointed One sent by God to rescue and redeem us into a right relationship with Him.

There is no more important question for humanity than "Who is Jesus?"

- **HOW WOULD YOU** answer that question if an unbeliever posed it to you?

- **WHAT KIND OF** triggers or situations tempt you to forget who Jesus truly is?

- **WHAT DOES LIFE** look like for you when you are undeniably certain that Jesus is the Christ? In contrast, what does it look like when you doubt this?

Day 77

GOD DOESN'T CALL AUDIBLES

*"Because I, the LORD, have not changed, you descendants of
Jacob have not been destroyed."* MALACHI 3:6

SINCE I'M IN MY early fifties I'm in the midst of drastic change. For instance, I've recently discovered I've been blessed with the gift of projective perspiration. My disloyal lady parts leapfrogged right over innocuous hot flashes and have chosen to participate in a lesser-known menopausal symptom called "volcanic eruptions." In other words, I sweat like a sumo wrestler in a sauna and typically do so at very inopportune times. Like at public functions or at four o'clock in the morning when I should be sleeping.

Such was the case a few weeks ago when I woke up before dawn wide-eyed and disoriented only to discover I was essentially floating in a pool of my own making. I groggily thought, *Okay, I can either lie here and let my frustration grow with each soggy passing second or I can go ahead and get up.* Then I mused, *I wonder if I drank some super-hot coffee if it would trick my body into cooling down?* Which is what ultimately compelled me to roll out of bed and stumble through the dark to the pantry rooting for java beans.

I found just enough coffee beans in the bottom of my last bag to make one single cup of go-go juice. So I decided I'd French-press the brew to perfection and then savor it peacefully while sitting at the kitchen island watching the sun come up at the same time my body temp would hopefully be going down. Unfortunately, when I carried my steaming cup of liquid joy to the island and began to sit down, I was so sweaty I slipped on the edge of the barstool and ended up spilling the coffee over a stack of papers in front of me.

Upon closer inspection, I discovered the ruined paperwork was Missy's homeschool lesson for the day (we're engaged in a "University-hybrid" educational program, tutoring, and classroom learning environments). Right then and there I made the executive decision to change her curriculum and move our schoolwork to the mall for a little lesson on capitalism. And I was almost sure I heard the Holy Spirit whisper that it was okay for us to drive through Starbucks on the way.

So when Missy woke up a few hours later, I used lots of enthusiastic inflection to inform her of our edited educational itinerary and quickly bundled her into the car for our soon-to-be caffeinated field trip. Unfortunately, my cropped-pants-wearing-barista was very grumpy and shoved my extra hot, non-fat mocha with whip (I choose to believe that non-fat milk and whipped cream cancel each other out making my drink choice almost healthy!) through the drive-thru window with a sniff of condescension. Frankly I think young men who choose to wear pants that end only a few inches below their knees have abdicated the right to be condescending, but that's because I'm old.

Anyway, I'm convinced Mr. Disdaining Short Pants *meant* to hand me a cup with an unsecured lid that would inevitably spill when I took it from him. I don't know how you react when you've already endured a very bad, no good, horrible morning and a cup of scalding hot coffee lands in your lap, but I accidentally blurted a word that's not in the Bible. I'm not proud of it, but I did it. Now I'm not going to tell you what the offensive word was, but I will confess it rhymed with "quit."

Sadly the incident went further downhill from there.

By now you know that since Missy is from Haiti, English is her second language. What you might not know is that as soon as I brought her home, she developed the habit of weaving new words into song melodies to help her remember them. So within a nanosecond of me blurting the bad word she'd woven it into one of her favorite tunes this season, which is Chris Tomlin's song "Good, Good Father."

Unfortunately, it only took another second or two for me to dig my pit of sin even deeper with the transgression of deception. I whirled around and exclaimed, "Oh no, baby, *that's* not the word Mama said! Mama said (at which point I sang these words to the same worship tune she'd just innocently warbled), 'You're a good, good coffee cup. So *sit* right here, *sit* right here.'" All while exaggerating the motion of taking the cup from the drive-thru window and placing it in the front seat cup holder.

Of course by the time we pulled into the Dillard's parking lot I felt like the worst Jesus-loving mom on the planet because it wasn't even lunchtime yet and I'd already led my sweet child into skipping school, said a bad word in front of her, and committed song piracy right here in our hometown of Music City. Suffice it to say, the immutability or *changelessness* of God has become one of my favorites of His attributes . . . because it's a trait noticeably missing from my life these days!

- **WHAT LIFE CHANGES** (hopefully not as dramatic or drippy as mine) have you disliked the most?

- **WHY WERE THOSE** particular transitions difficult for you to navigate?

- **IF YOU ARE** facing a season where things seem to be shifting around more than usual—whether in your circumstances or even your physical body!—how does God's changeless character encourage you?

Day 78
HELP IS ON THE WAY

"I will go before you and level the uneven places;
I will shatter the bronze doors and cut the iron bars in two.
I will give you the treasures of darkness and riches from secret places,
so that you may know that I am the LORD.
I am the God of Israel, who calls you by your name." ISAIAH 45:2–3

AS YOU HAVE PROBABLY figured out by now, many years ago, my sad-eyed, emaciated, almost-always coughing, daughter-to-be Missy was languishing in a Haitian orphanage, completely ignored by caregivers who were afraid of "catching" her HIV.

But today? Today my brave, almost-always laughing girl has more stamps in her passport than most adults. She's body surfed at Bondi Beach in Australia, gobbled fresh fish and chips in a London pub, hiked a snowy peak in New Zealand, watched a male lion slowly strut past on a South African safari, been baptized at the very same spot in the Jordan River where Scripture depicts Johnny B baptizing Jesus, and rolled her eyes in Edinburgh while I recited what was to her rather boring information about church history!

In little more than the blink of an eye, Melissa Price Harper transformed from ignored to adored, from barely surviving to thriving, from starving to satiated, from trapped to world traveler. And her vibrant transformation is solely due to our Savior's extravagant grace and mercy—His Spirit opened doors and closed gaps and provided protection and granted favor throughout our adoption journey. God alone made what man said was impossible, possible. Pretty much every time I gaze at my little girl, I'm reminded in a tangible, visceral way that *nothing* is too difficult for Him!

If you feel like you're at the end of your rope this season and wonder how in the world you're going to survive the difficult days still looming, I'm so sorry . . . I know what that feels like. But I'm delighted to report that Jesus really is a Waymaker and there will surely be miracles on the other side of this river of tears you're currently wading through. I don't know how He will answer, or if it will look the way you expected. Truth is, it probably won't! But I know this—*it will look just like He planned it to look* because His hands are always up to something good. So please *hang on,* cling to that knot at the end of your rope and don't you dare let Living Hope slip through your fingers because help is on the way!

- **WHAT FIGURATE "BRONZE** doors" or "iron bars" in your past—that you once despaired might be too big for even God to breach or break—did He shatter so that you could walk into the redemptive transformation He had for you?

- **WHAT OBSTACLES IN** your life currently appear insurmountable?

- **THINK ON GOD'S** past ability to make a way for you. In what ways does this memory give you the strength you need to believe He will do it again?

Day 79
SAYING NO TO STATUS QUO

Then Jesus said to his disciples, "If anyone wants to follow after me, let him deny himself, take up his cross, and follow me. For whoever wants to save his life will lose it, but whoever loses his life because of me will find it. For what will it benefit someone if he gains the whole world yet loses his life?" MATTHEW 16:24–26

I'M SURE YOU'VE HEARD of St. Francis of Assisi, who by all accounts was quite the Italian Stallion in his early, hard-partying days. However, according to his first biographer, after several transformational encounters with Christ, he sensed God telling him to repair "the church, which was in ruins."[14] So Francis pilfered some expensive cloth from his father's shop (his dad was a very wealthy merchant) and rode to a nearby village where he sold both the cloth and his horse. Then, when the town priest was reluctant to receive the funds, Francis hurled the cash out of a window.

Mind you, when his father found out about it, he was furious with Francis and brought him before their bishop to answer for the reckless embezzlement. But before the bishop had a chance to address him, Francis of Assisi stripped completely naked, handed his clothes to his shocked dad and announced: "Until now I have called you my father on earth. But henceforth I can truly say: *Our Father* who art in heaven."[15] Then he basically turned on his heel, hiked up into the mountains above his hometown, and devoted himself to a much simpler, mostly solitary life surrounded by animals instead of people.

Less well known than Saint Francis but every bit as passionate about forsaking anything or anyone who distracted them from their pursuit of Jesus was a group of Christians in the 1400s called the Stylites or "Pillar Saints" (after the Greek word *stulos*, which means pillar or column). Their extremely ascetic practice of moving away from community and making their homes atop pillars in the wilderness so as to avoid distractions and devote themselves entirely to God began in 423 BC by Simeon the Elder and continued until the mid-fifteenth century. One saint named Alypius is recorded as standing upright on a column less than four feet in diameter for fifty-three years until his ankles collapsed. However, instead of descending from his pillar and maybe going to a podiatrist, he laid down on his side and spent the last fourteen years of his life prone but still solitary, on his airy altar!

Now quite frankly, I think the Pillar Saints' "statuesque" acts of faith, while well intentioned, are totally bonkers. I've been studying Scripture for almost forty years and I'm pretty sure the Bible tells us to go and minister to other people and make disciples out of them, not run from them. I've yet to find a single verse that advocates hanging out alone on a glorified pole in order to please God! And unlike Assisi if I staged a nude protest, I'm pretty sure no one would call it an act of devotion. More likely probable cause for arrest! However, as totally bonkers as St. Francis and the Pillar Saints behavior seems to us now, I have to admit I admire their radical willingness to forgo comfort . . . to snub their noses at normalcy . . . to quash status quo for the sake of Christ.

- **WHAT CREATURE-COMFORTS DO** you typically run to instead of Christ? Why?

- **WHAT DOES JESUS'** command to "take up your cross" look like in the context of your life?

- **WHAT OR WHO** have you felt compelled to deny yourself of so as to be closer to God?

Day 80

KINDNESS ROCKS

"Therefore, whatever you want others to do for you, do also the same for them, for this is the Law and the Prophets." MATTHEW 7:12

— , · — — —

MISSY CONFESSED TO ME recently that she didn't want to go to day camp again because a couple days ago, a few of the other kids made fun of the way she talks. When the counselor was out of earshot, they told her she was dumb and accused her of cutting while they waited in line for the slide. Which led to a long conversation about how sometimes when people act ugly, it's really because they're scared or sad. So, we prayed for the kids who bullied her to feel safe so their hearts could grow big enough to fit joy and kindness in.

Then we practiced ways she could have clearer conversations and better engage with people she's meeting for the first time. She was so sweet while we role-played but at one point got frustrated after tripping over the same word twice, smacked herself in the forehead and blurted, "I'm sorry I talk funny, Mama." At which point I had to bite my lip to keep from crying while gently explaining that despite speech therapy, she might always speak English differently than people who grew up in America because she spent her early years in a different country with a completely different language called Creole. I encouraged her to keep working on her language skills, but said I thought her way of speaking English was lovely because it had a musical cadence.

She fixed her big brown eyes on mine and nodded soberly while I explained that some people will initially miss her heart because their first assessment of her will simply be that she's "different." However, once they get to know how awesome she actually is, they'd be crazy if they didn't want to be her friend. As you can imagine, I didn't sleep very well after putting Missy to bed. I just kept tossing and turning and praying for Jesus and His angel armies to protect the softest parts of my little girl from the sharpest edges of life.

We had another sweet conversation the next morning over breakfast and practiced "bringing out the best in bullies" again on the way to her day camp. But I'm telling you it was all I could do not to turn the car around and drive to some imaginary happy place where I could better protect her from the large rocks that sometimes even little people sling. Being Missy's mama is the most beautiful gift—second only to my relationship with Jesus—God has blessed me with. But it can still be a brutal kind of beautiful. And a poignant reminder to treat others the way I want to be treated—even more so, the way I want *my daughter* to be treated.

- **WHEN HAVE YOU** felt like the target of a bully throwing rocks?

- **DID ANY OF** the rocks connect with your heart? If so, how did you respond?

- **HAVE YOU EVER** prayed for the bullies in your life? Why or why not?

Day 81
STUMBLING SAINTS

Brothers and sisters, consider your calling: Not many were wise from a human perspective, not many powerful, not many of noble birth. Instead, God has chosen what is foolish in the world to shame the wise, and God has chosen what is weak in the world to shame the strong. God has chosen what is insignificant and despised in the world—what is viewed as nothing—to bring to nothing what is viewed as something, so that no one may boast in his presence. It is from him that you are in Christ Jesus, who became wisdom from God for us—our righteousness, sanctification, and redemption—in order that, as it is written: Let the one who boasts, boast in the Lord. 1 CORINTHIANS 1:26–31

―――――――――

THE FACT THAT JESUS picked Peter to lead the early church right before He ascended into heaven to sit at the right hand of God the Father makes my heart smile from ear to ear. Because remember this is the same knucklehead who threw Jesus—who was also his BFF—under the bus right before our Messiah's bogus arrest, horrific beating, and humiliating, painful death on a cross.

Pete, arguably the most yellow-bellied, Benedict Arnold in the entire Bible, is the highly unlikely dude our Savior passes the baton of spiritual leadership to. Instead of kicking him off the team after he fumbled the ball on the first yard line, Jesus appoints Peter to be team captain. Which proves that epic failures don't have the power to sabotage our futures because God's kingdom purposes have never been intrinsically linked to human capacity or a lack thereof. Whew!

So take a deep breath along with me, because nobody's going to miss out on a life-changing encounter with our Creator-Redeemer just because one of us makes a mistake during a Gospel presentation. Neither will He boot our hot mess selves to the curb. Instead Scripture reveals our divine King to be patient and kind, One who is slow to anger and great in mercy (Ps. 145:8)—basically One who picks us up after an inevitable failure, wipes the dirt off our face with a towel, then wraps the towel around the back of our neck to pull us into an awkwardly intimate forehead-to-forehead embrace. When we finally let go of enough shame to make eye contact, God winks and says, "You've got this!" Then I think maybe He rolls up the towel and teasingly snaps it behind us as we stride toward our destiny! Okay, obviously we can't find that anywhere in the Bible. But that's how I picture things going down!

The point is this: perfection is not a prerequisite to begin and remain in relationship with the Alpha and Omega! Additionally, the way God goes about choosing His ambassadors defies human logic: He equips adolescences to slay giants, prostitutes to save nations, one little kid's fish and chips lunch to feed a hungry multitude, and a team of twelve mostly rough-hewn and uneducated men—including a couple of guys He *knows* will throw shade—to reflect the Living Hope of the Gospel to the rest of the world!

If you look in a spiritual mirror long enough, you'll wince at the filthiness of your own clay feet . . . but you'll also begin to make out the outline of the nail-scarred ones you're standing on.

- **WHAT DEFICIT OR** defect in your life do you think God has utilized the most to reflect divine glory?

- **HOW HAVE YOU** seen Him use your most flawed moments to work kingdom wonders?

- **HOW DOES PETER'S** life encourage you in the seasons you've made major mistakes?

Day 82
WHEN SCARS BECOME BEAUTY MARKS

*Therefore, if anyone is in Christ, he is a new creation; the old has
passed away, and see, the new has come!* 2 CORINTHIANS 5:17

I GOT TO HANG out with Wonder Woman recently. Well, not Wonder Woman
exactly. Her name is Lori, not Gal Gadot (the actress in the 2017 blockbuster
film *Wonder Woman* and 20/21 follow up film, *Wonder Woman 1984*). But she's
incredibly brave despite her lack of knee-high red boots and a cape. Because
Lori just passed the three-month mark of being clean from heroin and methamphetamines after an eight-year addiction that culminated in her conviction
for illegal drug possession and armed robbery charges.

Unlike most of the women I meet at The Next Door (a six-month, faith-
based residential program that provides recovery support services for women
conquering their addictions to alcohol and drugs), Lori looks younger than her
age (she's twenty-three). The first time we met she was wearing a hoodie sweatshirt with a popular logo emblazoned on the front, torn jeans, and metallic
nail polish. As a matter of fact, if I'd seen her strolling through the mall or
giggling with her girlfriends in a coffee shop, I would've assumed she was a
happy-go-lucky college student. It wasn't until she pushed up the sleeves of
her sweatshirt, and I noticed the long, ragged scars from shooting up, that the
tragic reality of her former life became apparent.

Because I've had the privilege of volunteering with several addiction-recovery
programs, much of Lori's story is achingly familiar. She grew up in a very poor
family in a very small town. One of her parents moonlighted as a mean-spirited
bully, who claimed to be "knocking the stupid out of her" when smacking Lori
around. Of course, Lori wasn't stupid at all. Despite the regular beatings she
endured at home, she excelled in school. She made the honor roll and the cheerleading squad. After making an emotional commitment to Christ at a youth
rally, she became an outspoken Christian leader on campus.

However, when Lori's parents divorced, she became the sole possession of
her abuser, and her world caved in. She eventually ran away from home and

moved in with her boyfriend. He introduced her to methamphetamines, which numbed the searing pain of the compound fractures in her heart. And the rest, as they say, is history. Horrible, awful, gut-wrenching history.

That is until God intervened with a team of Tennessee-based federal agents wearing flak jackets. Lori's voice brightened when we were getting to know each other and she shared the part of her story where those law enforcement officers burst into her trailer to arrest her. She looked up at me through her bangs and grinned. Then she said with newfound confidence, "Miss Lisa, I *know* God ordained the exact timing of my drug bust, because I'd planned to commit suicide that afternoon. If those cops hadn't come when they did, I wouldn't be sitting here today."

Before I left, we talked about the Bible study we'll be doing every Wednesday night for the next three months until she has to report to prison to serve what will likely be a reduced sentence of about eighteen months. When we hugged good-bye, she whispered she wanted to be a Bible teacher too when she gets out. I whispered back that her testimony will plunge the divine sword in satan's chest even deeper, and be used to set captives free!

Lori's recovery will be a day-by-day, uphill journey, but I can totally picture her a few years from now standing in front of a room filled with wide-eyed young girls hanging on every word of God's redemption story in her life.

The older I get, the more convinced I am that admittedly flawed sinners are the most credible witnesses of the Gospel, because blemished believers can't *fake* moral superiority. Our scars make it glaringly apparent that we couldn't protect ourselves from harm. Authentic Christian warriors with scabby knees, bruised hearts, and even track-marked arms, who sometimes stumble yet always grab onto the arm of His Spirit in order to stand up again and again, exemplify the redemptive power of divine grace. We prove how miraculous and restorative the love of God really is. We *know* we can't make it by ourselves and we are only kept together because of the miraculous redemption King Jesus provided for us on the cross. Only *He* can take a wounded soul and make her Wonder Woman.

- **WHAT ARE A** few of the scars you could show the Lord now, instead of hiding them?

- **WOULD YOU DESCRIBE** all of your scars as "badges of honor"? Why or why not?

- **HOW HAVE YOU** seen Christ heal the wounds of your past? How has He freed you to share your story?

Day 83

THE IMPOSSIBILITY OF HIS ABSENCE

God is our refuge and strength, a helper who is always found in times of trouble.
Therefore we will not be afraid, though the earth trembles
and the mountains topple into the depths of the seas,
though its water roars and foams and the mountains quake with its turmoil. Selah
There is a river—its streams delight the city of God,
the holy dwelling place of the Most High.
God is within her; she will not be toppled. God will help her when the morning dawns.
Nations rage, kingdoms topple; the earth melts when he lifts his voice.
The LORD of Armies is with us; the God of Jacob is our stronghold. Selah PSALM 46:1–7

THERE WERE QUITE A few bumps in the road for Missy physically the first year I brought her home because of her HIV, ramifications of the malnutrition and tuberculosis she'd suffered from as a toddler, and a few other pre-existing medical issues. However, because of the audacious grace of God and the great medical care she received at Vanderbilt Children's Hospital in our hometown of Nashville, Tennessee, the past four years have been relatively smooth health-wise for my little girl. That is, until a few months ago when a lab result indicated there might be something seriously wrong with her kidneys, and we needed to come back to the hospital for more tests.

It's never been difficult for me to speak, teach, and write about God's sovereign goodness; I firmly believe in His compassion and would pretty much stake my own life on it. But I've found my firm belief in God's goodness can get a bit flaccid when my *child's* life is at stake. Needless to say, after the doctor soberly informed me that there was a problem with Missy's kidney function—which is not uncommon for children with HIV—I found myself begging God for mercy on her behalf. Had it not been for a few dear friends who figuratively carried me to the roof and lowered me to Jesus in prayer, I probably would've been consumed with worry. And when we went back to the hospital for another round of tests, it was all I could do not to swipe a stray scalpel, slice myself open, snag one of my old kidneys, and ask the doc, "Here, will this fluffy one fit in my baby girl?"

Of course, I burst into tears of relief and broke out into an unrhythmic boogie of gratitude a few hours later when I got the call that her kidney function was back to normal and that tests revealed what caused them to malfunction was much less serious than it initially appeared to be. Yet, I also found myself emotionally jarred by the thought that millions of people don't get the "everything's okay" call like I did. Instead they've been rocked to their very core with news like "the biopsy's malignant" or "the leukemia's back" or "the tumor's grown."

If you've found yourself buckling under the weight of a bad report recently regarding yourself or someone you love, I'm so sorry. I prayed for those of you who're dealing with heartbreaking medical issues earlier this very evening, as I watched my miraculously healthy eleven-year-old run across our property toward a beautiful sunset that I did *nothing* to deserve but God still delighted to give us. I don't understand why news comes to us in the waves that it does. I can't get my arms around why a sunset is in my yard while rain is in someone else's this very moment. And though this kidney thing ended up alright, I can't guarantee myself that rain isn't coming again our way at some point, just around the bend tomorrow, or the next year, or in the next twenty years. There's just no telling.

Ultimately, I can't quite wrap my mind around God's sovereign goodness or the fact that all the plans He has for us are *ultimately* for our good and His glory, but I'm determined to keep a white-knuckled faith-grip on these things being true. And I pray that you will, too. I pray that even as you read this our heavenly Father will bless you with a tangible sense of His comforting presence. That you will *know* He hasn't forgotten you and His providence will never take you to a place where His grace isn't sufficient. That you'll truly *believe* God is with you right there in the middle of it, rain or shine.

- **WHEN YOU LOOK** back over your life story, can you honestly recall a chapter that includes God's absence?

- **WHAT BAD NEWS** have you gotten recently? How can you remind yourself that God is with you in the rain?

- **IF YOU ARE** in a season of "beautiful sunsets," how can you use this season to minister well to those who may not be?

Day 84
THE DITCH ON EITHER SIDE OF THE GOSPEL

Jesus entered the synagogue again, and a man was there who had a shriveled hand. In order to accuse him, they were watching him closely to see whether he would heal him on the Sabbath. He told the man with the shriveled hand, "Stand before us." Then he said to them, "Is it lawful to do good on the Sabbath or to do evil, to save life or to kill?" But they were silent. After looking around at them with anger, he was grieved at the hardness of their hearts and told the man, "Stretch out your hand." So he stretched it out, and his hand was restored. Immediately the Pharisees went out and started plotting with the Herodians against him, how they might kill him. MARK 3:1–6

PHYSICALLY SPEAKING, I'VE BEEN in a "fluffy" season for over a decade now—interspersed with brief periods of leanness when I can actually feel my hip bones while lying down on my back. Therefore, I've been to multiple Weight Watchers and Jenny Craig "weigh-ins." And the one thing I've noticed is that no matter what the time of day or time of year, most of us wear as little as possible when we weigh in. It might be the middle of an ice storm in February but doggone it, I'm still going to wear the thinnest nylon running pants or shorts in my closet, a wisp of a T-shirt, and flip flops or shoes I can easy slip off. I don't even wear much jewelry on those terrible, horrible, no good, standing-on-the-scale-next-to-a-perky-weight-management-counselor days because Every. Single. Ounce. Counts!

Defining your relationship with God solely based on the Law can be just as depressing because Every. Single. Infraction. Counts. Every impatient word in traffic. Every unkind thought in a slow checkout line at the grocery store. Every lapse in judgment. Every minute of insecurity. They all add up to tip the scale toward fantastically flawed. There is simply no such thing as a perfectly law-abiding human. Paul says it bluntly and succinctly in Romans chapter 3: "For all have sinned, and come short of the glory of God" (Rom. 3:23 KJV).

It's no wonder the Pharisees were grouchy; they were surely emotionally, physically, and mentally exhausted from trying to uphold the facade of moral perfection! Sadly, instead of owning up to their faults and receiving forgiveness and healing from the One who already knew the truth about them anyway, their hard hearts withered to the point of conspiring with the Herodians to kill Jesus.

The fact that the Pharisees and the Herodians—basically the biblical version of the Hatfields and McCoys—put aside their huge animosity toward each other so as to form an alliance against Jesus is significant. The Herodians represented the ruling power and hedonistic culture of Rome. Which means they were pluralistic, polytheistic pagans. They pretty much acted like entitled fraternity boys with fat wallets and no scruples. Which means they were the absolute opposite of the pursed-lipped, allergic-to-fun, law-abiding Pharisees.

These two crews coming together to take down the Son of God is as radical a concept as the leaders of the red states and the leaders of the blue states coming together to back the same presidential candidate. It highlights the shocking similarity between unrestrained immorality—*I'm going to do whatever feels good to me in the moment!*—and restrained moral conformity—*I'm going to follow the rules better than anyone else even if it kills me!* In both cases, the practitioner is attempting to be their own god. And both approaches lead to self-righteousness, to an ironic "we're so much better than people who think they're better than other people" type of arrogance. Yet all the while, both sides are just adding more and more weight to the scale of sin. Praise heaven for Jesus, who did away with all our sin, whatever form we tend to lean into!

- **WHAT SIMILAR PERSONALITY** traits have you noticed in modern-day Pharisees and wild-as-a-buck partiers who avoid Christianity like the plague?

- **WHICH EXTREME—RELIGIOSITY OR** secularism—do you tend to gravitate toward if you're not careful?

- **HOW ARE THE** sins of legalists and the sin of hedonists surprisingly alike?

Day 85
WORTH THE RISK

"But I say to you who listen: Love your enemies, do what is good to those who hate you, bless those who curse you, pray for those who mistreat you. If anyone hits you on the cheek, offer the other also. And if anyone takes away your coat, don't hold back your shirt either. Give to everyone who asks you, and from someone who takes your things, don't ask for them back. Just as you want others to do for you, do the same for them. If you love those who love you, what credit is that to you? Even sinners love those who love them. If you do what is good to those who are good to you, what credit is that to you? Even sinners do that. And if you lend to those from whom you expect to receive, what credit is that to you? Even sinners lend to sinners to be repaid in full. But love your enemies, do what is good, and lend, expecting nothing in return. Then your reward will be great, and you will be children of the Most High. For he is gracious to the ungrateful and evil. Be merciful, just as your Father also is merciful." LUKE 6:27–36

I'M OFTEN ASKED IF it's hard taking Missy back to Haiti to reestablish connections with her relatives and former caretakers—most of whom she barely remembers and a few of whom have falsely and manipulatively claimed to have cared for her back when she was a baby in the hopes of financial gain now. To answer that question honestly, yes, it's been super-hard. And really messy. And very emotionally draining. As well as, much more complicated than I initially anticipated, despite receiving lots of professional counseling and seeking the advice of social workers, child psychiatrists, and adoption specialists regarding this very issue.

Unfortunately, there is no perfect, fail-safe, step-by-step plan to follow when it comes to the process of restoration in the midst of the really heavy, complicated fallenness of the world. To sew love where there has been devastating loss is not unlike hiking uphill in the rain wearing a blindfold. However, for those stubbornly hopeful few who choose to attempt this proverbial hike, the view from the top is incomparably glorious. And for our little family the uphill climb of reconnecting with Missy's biological relatives and keeping her Haitian roots intact wasn't a risky option we could refuse because the Holy Spirit made it clear to me that it was a directive from my heavenly Father. Who, of course, knew before the beginning of time that it would bless my kid with a beautifully diverse well of affirmation and affection.

Plus, Missy's learning that while extending love and kindness isn't always an easy plan to navigate, it's always the *right* plan. Call me crazy, but I still believe that true love and real relationships are more than worth the high price of admission, and I hope my daughter grows up to be just as crazy as her Mama Blan. Sir C. S. Lewis says it best:

> To love at all is to be vulnerable. Love anything and your heart will be wrung and possibly broken. If you want to make sure of keeping it intact you must give it to no one, not even an animal. Wrap it carefully round with hobbies and little luxuries; avoid all entanglements. Lock it up safe in the casket or coffin of your selfishness. But in that casket, safe, dark, motionless, airless, it will change. It will not be broken; it will become unbreakable, impenetrable, irredeemable. To love is to be vulnerable.[16]

- **LUKE 6:27–36 CALLS** us to love hard even when it is hard. How has this paid relational dividends in your life?

- **IN WHAT WAYS** has God asked you to seek restoration and reconciliation in a messy relationship?

- **HOW DID GOD** seek restoration and reconciliation with you when you were in a broken relationship with Him? How does this change the way you view the broken or difficult relationships in your own life?

Day 86

BABY SEEDS AND BIG REVIVALS

"Because of your little faith," he told them. "For truly I tell you, if you have faith the size of a mustard seed, you will tell this mountain, 'Move from here to there,' and it will move. Nothing will be impossible for you." MATTHEW 17:20

I LOVE THAT JESUS uses a *mustard seed*—the smallest seed known to man and sown in agriculturally-oriented Israel—to illustrate the power of faith. It gives me, a woman whose faith sometimes shrinks to about that same dinky dimension, great hope.

A few months ago, my dear friend Paige and I were nearing the end of a long hike in Radnor Lake State Park, and although it had been an uncomfortably hot and humid day, my steps were still bouncier than when we started walking. Because about midway through the hike I'd confessed a crooked place in my heart and Paige had encouraged me with a familiar (but powerful!) biblical reminder—"he who began a good work in you will carry it on to completion until the day of Christ Jesus" (Phil. 1:6 NIV).

She'd reminded me that although sometimes I feel about as stable as a top-heavy Christmas tree in a stand with one screw, God *will* be faithful to complete what He began in my heart forty-plus years ago when I walked an aisle in a small Baptist church and gave my heart to Jesus.

Then, just about the time I was going to joyfully challenge her to a race since we only had about a quarter mile to go, I looked up to see a physician I've known for about twenty years walking toward us with sadness etched across his face. He seemed startled when I greeted him, and then it was as if seeing someone familiar knocked the stool of propriety out from under him, because huge tears began rolling down his face.

After we asked a few gentle questions, he explained that he was devastated over the death of his dad and it had caused a lot of soul-searching, which eventually led to him questioning his own worth as a man. His broad shoulders and voice literally shook when he said, "I know God loves me and all but when I look back over the course of my life, I don't feel like I've got anything significant to show for it and I'm afraid He's disappointed in me."

Largely because I was still floating on my own little cloud of spiritual refreshment, I looked directly into his eyes and asked boldly, "Dr. Smith (not his real name, of course), may we pray for you *right now*?" When he nodded in agreement (he probably didn't think he had much of a choice in the matter), Paige and I went to town! I mean we prayed heaven *down* on that dear man! All the while other hikers were walking past wide-eyed and giving us a huge berth, Paige and I were bellowing God's promises with glad authority:

> For He created your inmost being, Dr. Smith! He knit you together in your mama's womb. You are fearfully and wonderfully made because God's works are wonderful—we know that full well. (Ps. 139:13–14 RLV Radnor Lake Version, as we like to call it)

> He's close to the broken-hearted, Dr. Smith. Especially on days like today when you feel crushed, you can count on God's presence. (Ps. 34:18 RLV)

> You can hold your head UP, Dr. Smith, because there's now therefore no shame or condemnation for those of us who've put our hope in Jesus Christ! (Rom. 8:1 RLV)

By the time we said "Amen," Dr. Smith wasn't crying anymore, and we were all wearing revival grins. You can't tell me our God doesn't make majestic, praiseworthy mountains out of mere mustard seeds because I've seen it happen!

- **ON A SCALE** of 1 to 10, with 1 being a mustard seed and 10 being a watermelon, how would you rate the size of your faith this season?

- **HOW HAVE YOU** seen God use a granule of your faith for good?

- **WHO IN YOUR** life might need reminding that God will complete His good work in them?

Day 87

THE FELLOWSHIP OF TEARS

Rejoice with those who rejoice; weep with those who weep. Live in harmony with one another. Do not be proud; instead, associate with the humble. ROMANS 12:15–16

SOON AFTER MY PARENTS divorced, Dad Harper remarried and moved out of the city to forty-two acres of flat, cactus-dotted pastureland in Central Florida to begin his dream of becoming a cattleman-rancher. Before the moving boxes were all unpacked, Dad took me to the feed store to pick out my very first saddle—a beautiful, hand-tooled leather model with fancy silver concha decorations. I was so proud of that saddle and even more proud when the storeowner winked at Dad and asked, "Is this your new ranch-hand, Everett?" And Dad said, "Yep, she sure is!" Then, when he put his big hand on my little girl shoulder as we were walking out to the truck and said he was really going to need my help with our new cattle operation, I stretched at least an inch or two taller!

I'm sure I was more nuisance than asset those first few years of working cows with Dad. I wasn't big enough to hold them still for vaccinations and wasn't yet strong enough to circle a rope over my shoulder and lasso a calf while riding my beloved horse Gypsy, even though I practiced roping fence-posts by the barn every single weekend I got to be with Dad! Despite my ineptitude, I fell madly in love with taking care of our farm animals which included all manner of horses, cows, pigs, hens, dogs, and even a mean old rooster who angrily chased my stepbrother and me on a regular basis!

So one summer, when one of our mama cows died before weaning her calf and Dad asked me to nurse her calf with a bottle until it got strong enough to fend for itself, I was thrilled. I named the solid black, orphaned calf "Inky" and spent every waking moment tending to him. It wasn't long before that baby Hereford bonded to me, and pretty soon he no longer stayed in the pasture with the rest of the herd, but instead followed me around like an oversized puppy. He even started sleeping outside the house, curled up in the wobbly circle of our other snoring dogs, who completely accepted Inky despite the fact that he mooed instead of barked.

When my sweet baby bull was about a year old, Dad told me it was time to assimilate him back into the pasture with the rest of the cows. I cried, insisting that he didn't know how to be a cow anymore because he'd become part of our family. But when Dad gently encouraged me that we had to do what was best for Inky, I relented, knowing deep in my heart that he needed to be with his *real* family. (Although I still made several visits to the fence every day I was at Dad's to rub his growing black head and feed him treats.)

Not too long after we transitioned him from pet back to farm animal, a pack of rabid dogs attacked and killed several newborn calves and young cows at our neighbor's ranch and several of ours, including Inky. Dad teared up when he told me, explaining sorrowfully that even though Inky was a yearling and big enough to defend himself, he probably didn't because he thought of dogs as friends not as potentially dangerous.

I was crushed. After seeing his remains when my less-than-tender step-mother drove me down to the pasture while Dad was on the tractor trying to bury the corpses, I was inconsolable. I sobbed and sobbed, devastated by the realization that had I not turned Inky into a pet, he never would've been savagely attacked and killed. I couldn't help imagining him trotting over to that pack of wild dogs with his bright eyes and friendly disposition, assuming they wanted to play with him like our other dogs always did.

When Dad came up from the barn to clean up, my stepmother announced in an irritated huff that she was leaving to go shopping in town because she was sick of hearing me cry and carry on over a *stupid cow*. That mini tragedy took place when I was eleven years old and it's the first time (although certainly not the last) it occurred to me that grief is not an inclusive kind of emotion. That deep ache tends to be an isolating event. That despair tends to put uncomfortable distance between the heartbroken and observers. Especially if the observers haven't healthily processed their own grief and loss.

Thankfully, God doesn't leave us alone in our pain, or consider us stupid for feeling it in the depths of our soul. He doesn't stand at a distance whether we are in joy or grief. He weeps with us when our cheeks are soaked with tears, and He rejoices when we are brimming with joy. He bears it all right there beside us.

- **WOULD YOU DESCRIBE** the most painful season of your life as a lonely time? Why or why not?

- **WHY DO YOU** tend to think God wants distance from you when you are grieving?

- **WHAT CURRENT PAIN** are you facing right now, and how can you invite God into it?

Day 88
INVISIBLE IS NOT YOUR MIDDLE NAME

You will be a glorious crown in the LORD's hand,
and a royal diadem in the palm of your God's hand.
You will no longer be called Deserted,
and your land will not be called Desolate;
instead, you will be called My Delight Is in Her,
and your land Married;
for the LORD delights in you,
and your land will be married. ISAIAH 62:3–4

IN HIS CLASSIC BOOK *Counterfeit Gods,* Tim Keller wrote: "If we look to some created thing to give us the meaning, hope, and happiness that only God himself can give, it will eventually fail to deliver and break our hearts."[17] But boy that truism is sometimes like wet soap to me—it's hard to hang onto.

For the better part of my adult life, Mother's Day weekend was a painful reminder that I didn't have a family of my own. Mind you, I tried not to act sad because I genuinely wanted to celebrate my sweet mama as well as the majority of my friends who have children. But there were hard moments when the act was hard to keep up, like when the ushers at church handed out roses to all the moms entering the sanctuary and I just smiled and shook my head "no" when they started to hand me a bloom, hoping my broken heart wasn't too obvious as I walked past with what I hoped appeared to be a pleasant expression and willing myself not to tear up.

By the time I was in my forties I'd come to recognize and grieve the fact that my singleness was the direct result of my sinful choices, relational toxicity, and rebellion. Yet while repentance brought deeper peace with God and much healthier relationship patterns, it did not cause a prince to magically appear with a glass slipper that fit my middle-aged feet, nor did my womb revert to youthful elasticity like Sarah's. It's purely by God's redemptive kindness that I now get handmade cards from my daughter on Mother's Day, and while Missy's love means more than I can express, I think I'll always be mindful of the women who feel quiet despair on Mother's Day.

So at the risk of meddling or sounding like some perky weight-loss coach who *used* to be pudgy, I encourage those of you who long for children of your own to love to marinate in these tangible promises of the One *who has not forgotten you*:

God sets the lonely in families. (Ps. 68:6a NIV)

"Rejoice, childless one, who did not give birth;
burst into song and shout,
you who have not been in labor!
For the children of the desolate one will be more
than the children of the married woman,"
says the LORD.
"Enlarge the site of your tent,
and let your tent curtains be stretched out;
do not hold back;
lengthen your ropes,
and drive your pegs deep.
For you will spread out to the right and to the left,
and your descendants will dispossess nations
and inhabit the desolate cities." (Isa. 54:1–3)

And for what it's worth, sometimes I gave myself a pass on Mother's Day and skipped church, drove to Starbucks and ordered a mocha Frappuccino with extra whipped cream, then drove aimlessly down country roads with the sunroof open while blasting '80s pop tunes. It really did help lessen the sting a bit.

- **WHAT DATE ON** the calendar or yearly anniversary always seems to make you feel invisible?

- **WHAT LIFE STAGE** are you tempted to think equates with "making it"?

- **WHY DO YOU** think achieving this life stage—or rather, not achieving it—has the power to make you feel despair? How has God proven Himself to be enough in past moments of despair?

Day 89

GOD DOESN'T NEED GPS

When they approached Jerusalem, at Bethphage and Bethany near the Mount of Olives, he sent two of his disciples and told them, "Go into the village ahead of you. As soon as you enter it, you will find a colt tied there, on which no one has ever sat. Untie it and bring it. If anyone says to you, 'Why are you doing this?' say, 'The Lord needs it and will send it back here right away.'" MARK 11:1–3

THE FACT THAT JESUS begins His descent toward that very first Easter from the Mount of Olives is hugely significant. It rises dramatically, less than a mile away, and directly east of Jerusalem. It's the same historic hill where our Savior later prophesied that He would return a second time (Acts 1:10–11), which the ancient prophet Zechariah had prophesied about in detail centuries before:

> On that day his feet will stand on the Mount of Olives, which faces Jerusalem on the east. The Mount of Olives will be split in half from east to west, forming a huge valley, so that half the mountain will move to the north and half to the south. You will flee by my mountain valley, for the valley of the mountains will extend to Azal. You will flee as you fled from the earthquake in the days of King Uzziah of Judah. Then the LORD my God will come and all the holy ones with him. (Zech. 14:4–5)

It's also hugely significant that Jesus humbly chose to ride an untrained colt instead of an impressive warhorse down that olive-tree dotted hillside. Because it's a dead giveaway that He's not the kind of military-minded king most Jews were hoping for, who would defeat their human oppressors and return Israel to its former geo-political glory. Plus, it fulfills another Old Testament prophecy:

> Rejoice greatly, Daughter Zion!
> Shout in triumph, Daughter Jerusalem!
> Look, your King is coming to you;
> he is righteous and victorious,

humble and riding on a donkey,
on a colt, the foal of a donkey.
(Zech. 9:9)

Although the disciples were pretty much clueless as to the redemptive drama that was about to unfold (despite having been told what was going to happen three times already by Jesus Himself!), every single detail of that pre-Easter passion parade unfolded exactly according to God's plan. And I shouldn't be poking fun at Jesus' first-century posse, because I'm a slow spiritual learner, too! It's taken me a really long time to learn to trust God when I can't see around the corner of my circumstances. Or when what I can see doesn't make sense to me. Yet the further I stumble along on this walk of faith toward deeper intimacy with Him, the more convinced I am that God is the only perfect and eternal cartographer.

- **THE CROWD'S SHOUTS** of "Hosanna" when Jesus entered Jerusalem literally meant, "Save, I pray!" and are loosely translated, "Lord, save us!" Unfortunately, they were asking to be saved from their political/financial/ social oppression and not from the eternally damning consequences of their sin. How and when have you begged God to save you from the wrong thing?

- **WHEN YOU CAN'T** see what's ahead, how do you usually try to strategize or forecast?

- **HOW ARE YOU** like the disciples in this story when it comes to your expectation of Jesus?

Day 90
LAUGHING IN THE LOUVRE

Now faith is the assurance of things hoped for,
the conviction of things not seen. HEBREWS 11:1 ESV

———

IF YOU'D TOLD ME seventeen years ago that one day I'd get to visit Paris with my daughter, I'd have thought quietly to myself that you were probably off your rocker. If you'd told me seventeen years ago that one day my daughter would look up at me with a twinkle in her big, beautiful brown eyes after viewing the actual *Mona Lisa* painting in the Louvre and exclaim, "Mom, this is *awesome!*", I'd have questioned out loud if you'd been smoking something medicinal. I just couldn't imagine as a forty-year-old single woman lugging a past full of foolish choices that God would lavish me with the underserved gift of motherhood when I was fifty years old. To my pre-adoption-miracle ears that would've sounded like trying to catch a Hail Mary pass on a snowy Saturday wearing gloves slathered in mayonnaise!

At forty, I simply couldn't allow myself to dream of a future with enough restoration in it to include a family of my own. Not after more than a decade of whopper relational mistakes on my end. By then I didn't think I could deal with what I assumed would inevitably be crushing disappointment. When you've lived the "hope deferred makes the heart sick" aspect of Proverbs 13, it's hard to hang onto the "a desire fulfilled is a tree of life" part. So I learned to effectively pour cold water on the embers of hope in my own heart that someday a child might call me "Mama," or that someday I might get to shop for colored binders and thick reams of notepaper and Elmer's glue so that my child's backpack would be filled with all the requisite items necessary for their first day of school, or that someday there might be a stocking with a child's name embroidered across the top hung on my fireplace mantel at Christmastime.

Even though I brought her home from Haiti quite a few years ago now, I'm still tempted to pinch myself that this extraordinary little girl calls me "Mama." That I have the pure joy of walking down the school supply aisles in Target with my chattering daughter every August now and can't help but smile when she asks sweetly if she can pretty please get a pink binder—even though it's not one of the required colors—because it's her most favorite color ever. And the fact that we hung up those hand-embroidered stockings with the names "Missy" and "Mom" on our fireplace mantel a little later than usual this year didn't make me heartsick either because we got to spend the last week in November—when we normally decorate our home for Christmas—in Paris where I watched the child I'd all but given up hoping for skip down the marble hallways of the Louvre after consuming a chocolate crepe bigger than her head from a sidewalk vendor who proclaimed sincerely, "Madame, your daughter is trés belle!" as I was counting out the francs to pay him.

I don't have the energy to guard my heart from disappointment anymore because I'm far too busy being gobsmacked by God's redemptive kindness. That doesn't mean disappointment never comes to my door. It just means that our Creator-Redeemer is up to, well, *redeeming* things in our lives, and when our eyes focus intently on the ways He's doing that, the disappointments pale in comparison.

- **WHAT/WHO IS THE** biggest example of God's redemptive kindness in your life?

- **WHERE ARE YOU** pouring cold water on hope?

- **HOW CAN YOU** intentionally start praising God for all He is redeeming in your life?

Day 91
CATCHING HORNETS WITH HONEY

A gentle answer turns away anger,
but a harsh word stirs up wrath.
The tongue of the wise makes knowledge attractive,
but the mouth of fools blurts out foolishness.
The eyes of the LORD are everywhere,
observing the wicked and the good.
The tongue that heals is a tree of life,
but a devious tongue breaks the spirit. PROVERBS 15:1–4

DEAR WOMAN WHO KEEPS sending me unkind messages about Missy dancing in public because of my bad parenting skills,

My daughter often borrows my phone and recently, she accidentally clicked on your latest anonymous indictment about us before I realized what she was up to. I could tell it wounded her little girl spirit when she looked up and asked softly, "Mama, why is this lady being so mean about me dancing with Aunt Chris?"

I told her that you were probably a lot like the Grinch—that you probably didn't receive as much love as you deserved when you were little, or maybe your heart had been hurt so badly that you felt like you had no choice but to keep it small and hard so it wouldn't get kicked around again. To which she replied that we should love you more then, because when the Grinch was loved, his heart grew and all the grumpiness got pushed out.

So I want to inform you that Missy and I are now praying for you on a daily basis—believing for God to send people into your life who see past your likely self-protective veneer to the image-bearer inside who is so worthy of healthy love and friendship and belonging.

And since you described Missy's dancing as "an inappropriate, attention-seeking public spectacle," she wanted you to know that she dances all the time in private too. When I asked her why a few years ago, she explained simply, "Mama, I like to dance . . . it makes me feel happy."

Given the fact that doctors in Haiti only gave my daughter a few months to live after her first mama died when she was a baby and she languished in an orphanage long after that horrific loss, I believe Missy's very life is a miracle and her joyful, always-ready-to-dance personality is the supernatural way God wired her to defy the natural odds.

Now you're obviously entitled to your own opinion and if her dancing continues to offend you, please unfollow me asap for your own peace of mind, especially in light of the fact that this isn't the first time you've aired your grievances on the Internet.

Finally, please know the video attached to this note is a recording my miracle kid choreographed especially for you, smack-dab in the middle of our five acres in the boonies of Tennessee where no one else besides me could see—or appreciate—her sheer joy.

It's not about garnering attention, ma'am, it's about exulting in being alive.

Sincerely,
Lisa Harper (a.k.a.: Missy's mom)

- **WHEN'S THE LAST** time you sloshed grace on a stinker whose behavior deserved a good tongue-lashing?

- **HOW DID YOUR** gentle response affect your relationship with said stinker?

- **WHEN HAS SOMEONE** else's gentle answer effectively "turned away" your anger?

Day 92

THE HIGHEST LOW

Jesus called them over and said to them, "You know that those who are regarded as rulers of the Gentiles lord it over them, and those in high positions act as tyrants over them. But it is not so among you. On the contrary, whoever wants to become great among you will be your servant, and whoever wants to be first among you will be a slave to all. For even the Son of Man did not come to be served, but to serve, and to give his life as a ransom for many." MARK 10:42–45

NOT TOO LONG AGO I had the honor and privilege of addressing a group of several hundred recovering addicts. Most of them were recovering from some type of substance abuse, like alcohol or opioids, and a few were recovering from various forms of sexual addiction and deviance. All of them were unflinchingly honest. And within a few hours, most of them seemed like old friends.

I've had an affinity for people in addiction recovery since I first began volunteering at homeless shelters with my Dad Harper when I was in high school. I couldn't quite put a finger on why I resonated with that particular people group until decades later when I was in seminary and read a book titled, *Addictions: A Banquet in the Grave* by Dr. Edward T. Welch, which includes the profound assertion and challenge: "Addictions are ultimately a disorder of worship. Will we worship ourselves and our own desires, or will we worship the true God?"[18]

And that's when it hit me: *I'm a recovering addict too.* Because the basic takeaway of Dr. Welch's thoroughly-researched and superbly written book is that when we don't put Jesus in the deepest hole in our soul, we will *all* attempt to put people or substances in a void that was created by God for Christ alone. While I've never struggled with an alcohol or drug addiction, nor lost my teeth to meth or been incarcerated, I did spend years emotionally imprisoned by the seemingly innocuous, less-obvious addictions of engaging in abusive romantic relationships and desperately trying to earn the approval of others. The consequences of my addictions weren't as outwardly devastating or illegal, but at the heart level they were still debilitating. And just like my now sober friends who were once addicted to crack, meth, alcohol or hydrocodone, I too used to act like a sick puppy foolishly licking antifreeze off the garage floor, unaware it had the power to kill me.

Suffice it to say, getting to keynote at that conference for recovering addicts for me was like a peewee football player getting to do warm-up drills with the pros. These warriors had made it through the hardest of challenges—much harder than mine in so many ways—so who was I to speak to them about anything? The experience was both thrilling and humbling. Although I didn't know just *how* humbling the experience would be until what happened after I spoke and walked back to my seat in the sanctuary. Because that's when a woman approached without fanfare, knelt down by my feet, slipped off my shoes one at a time, gently cleaned them with a Wet-Wipe, and then massaged them tenderly with oil from a small vial she pulled out of her tattered purse.

I've had my feet washed before as part of an organized group object lesson on servant leadership but that was different. That was a shared activity where all the participants knew each other, and we all knew what to expect. Plus, we took turns, so the humbling element was dissipated by the familiarity and the give-and-take of the exercise. But there was no give-and-take this time and I'd only met the foot-washing lady briefly that morning.

I was so flustered at first that I tried to pull my foot away from her, mumbling something about it being nice but not necessary. However, when she looked up kindly while holding my foot firmly and said sincerely, "Please let me do this for you." I swallowed the "I'm not worthy" shame that had erupted in my heart and mind and yielded to her nurturing. Before long huge tears were rolling down my face because I was so overwhelmed by how she had minimized herself in order to minister to me.

- **WHEN IT COMES** to humble acts of service—whether it's washing someone's feet or washing someone's dishes who's bedridden with a serious illness—are you more comfortable being on the giving end or on the receiving end?

- **WHERE DO YOU** feel inadequate or unworthy to serve?

- **WHY DOES GOD** typically use the unlikely or inadequate to minister in His name?

Day 93

AGGRESSIVE GRACE

"When he came to his senses, he said, 'How many of my father's hired servants have food to spare, and here I am starving to death! I will set out and go back to my father and say to him: Father, I have sinned against heaven and against you. I am no longer worthy to be called your son; make me like one of your hired servants.' So he got up and went to his father. But while he was still a long way off, his father saw him and was filled with compassion for him; he ran to his son, threw his arms around him and kissed him. The son said to him, 'Father, I have sinned against heaven and against you. I am no longer worthy to be called your son.' But the father said to his servants, 'Quick! Bring the best robe and put it on him. Put a ring on his finger and sandals on his feet!'" LUKE 15:17–22 NIV

———

SEVERAL YEARS AGO, WHEN I was stressed over being so far behind on a book deadline, I was sitting at the kitchen table typing and realized my cell phone wasn't next to my laptop, where I was pretty sure I'd left it. Missy was comfortably sprawled out on the couch about twenty feet away watching *The Fox and the Hound* (which used to be one of her favorite Disney classics), so I called out, "Hey honey, have you seen my phone?" To which she chirped happily, "Yes ma'am!" I got up from the table and walked over to her and asked, "Baby, I need to check something on my phone so will you please tell me where it is?" She grinned mischievously and replied, "I put it in a draweh, Mama!"

I wasn't feeling especially tolerant at the time but realizing she thought we were playing a game, I tried to play along, "Okay, baby, how about you show me what drawer you chose to hide Mama's phone in?" She bounced to her feet and began skipping from room to room, opening drawer after drawer, none of which contained my phone.

After about fifteen minutes of the increasingly frustrating routine of Missy emphatically declaring, "It's in *'dis* drawah, Mama!" only to find that it wasn't, and after I'd stopped the festivities several times to clarify how important it was for her to show me where she'd hidden my phone (Missy had only been speaking English for about a year at that point so there was still a significant communication gap between us), I reached the bottom of my patient parent bucket.

I knelt down to her level, looked directly into her beautiful brown eyes, and said in a very firm tone that sounds shockingly like the one my mother used with me when I misbehaved at Missy's age, "Melissa, This. Is. Not. Funny. At. All. If you don't show me where you put my phone *right now*, I will turn off the movie and you're going to bed early." Of course, her eyes filled with crocodile tears and her bottom lip began to tremble but since I think consistency is critical in parenting, I followed through by putting my hand on her tiny shoulder and herding her to her bedroom, turning the TV off en route much to her dismay.

A little while later, I came trudging back downstairs with a sagging spirit because I don't enjoy disciplining Missy even though I know it's usually for her good. Plus, I was fretting about the fact that I didn't have time to go to the Apple store to get a new phone the next day, not to mention dreading what crucial data might have been gobbled from my iPhone innards never to seen again by the ubiquitous, carnivorous "cloud."

Frustration and worry were getting their party started in my head when I glanced at the Bible next to my laptop and wondered, "What is that weird lump in my study Bible?" Before I flipped it open to find the "missing" phone, my heart had already begun it's swift descent to my stomach. It's a wonder the Holy Spirit didn't zap my posterior with lightning as I bolted back upstairs to Missy's room in order to apologize.

I sat down on the edge of her bed and took her hand in mine, but before I was able to explain why I was sorry, her face split into a grin, she blurted out sincerely, "Dat's okay, Mama. I lub you!" wrapped her arms around me, and squeezed. My tenderhearted baby girl is so uncomfortable when she feels distance between us that she often jumps the gun and forgives me before I even have time to confess!

The thing that slays me about the story of the prodigal son is that the father forgave the son before the wayward dude even began to *repent!* He wraps his arms around his son before the son can even start his speech! So does that mean repentance isn't an important thing when it comes to genuine salvation? Nope. It means that the father was so incredibly eager to restore the son into a right relationship with himself that he preempted the son's true repentance (which our Father *knows beforehand* because He's *omnipotent*) with mercy. I don't know about you, but the idea of our Father jumping the gun and forgiving me before I even confess—actually *pursuing* me with aggressive grace—puts me in the mood to admit my mistakes much faster!

- **HOW CAN YOU** relate to the prodigal son in this passage?

- **IN YOUR MOMENTS** of stumbling, how does it make you feel to know that God is—instead of fuming or apathetic—uncomfortable with and even saddened about the distance between the two of you?

- **HAS IT EVER** occurred to you that when you run to God to repent, He's actually been running toward you the whole time, too?

Day 94

THE GIRL NO ONE WANTED

But Mary stood outside the tomb, crying. As she was crying, she stooped to look into the tomb. She saw two angels in white sitting where Jesus's body had been lying, one at the head and the other at the feet. They said to her, "Woman, why are you crying?" "Because they've taken away my Lord," she told them, "and I don't know where they've put him." Having said this, she turned around and saw Jesus standing there, but she did not know it was Jesus. "Woman," Jesus said to her, "why are you crying? Who is it that you're seeking?" Supposing he was the gardener, she replied, "Sir, if you've carried him away, tell me where you've put him, and I will take him away." Jesus said to her, "Mary." Turning around, she said to him in Aramaic, "Rabboni!"—which means "Teacher." JOHN 20:11–16

———

A FORMER DEMONIAC, MARY from Magdala (*Magdala* means "fish tower" and is the name of the unimpressive fishing village Mary grew up in) was the very first person to see the risen Messiah. Which surely caused more than a few to cry, "FOUL!" Plenty of folks probably raised their eyebrows and wondered, "Is she really the *best* spokesperson for the resurrection of our Lord Jesus?" I'd be willing to bet good money on the fact that some women in that first-century audience made snide remarks about Mary's less-than-trendy outfit. And based on their initial dismissal of her claim (Mark 16:11; Luke 24:10–11), even the disciples, who'd known Mary for years, seemed to think the cause of Christ would be far better off with a more credible eyewitness to Easter.

Now their resistance to Mary's leading role in the Passion Play stands to reason because based on the number of demons Jesus cast out of her (Luke 8:1–2 tells us there were seven, a number that illustrates completion in biblical literature), the disciples likely assumed she'd been *completely* oppressed by satan. Which means basically by the time Mary was a freshman at Magdala High she was an outcast. She didn't smile much. She didn't participate in classroom conversations. She didn't make the cheerleading squad. She sat by herself in the lunchroom. And she definitely didn't get invited to prom. I mean good night, what mama wants her darling teenaged son to take a nutjob to that pivotal shindig of adolescence? Mary had probably been branded as "less than the best choice" by pretty much everybody in Magdala before she even got her driver's license.

John Ortberg describes the resurrection as "the fulcrum of the Christian faith." In other words, our entire belief system hinges on Easter—on the fact that our Savior didn't stay dead. And don't forget, our Creator-Redeemer is a God of details—He put stripes on zebras and gave cells their nucleus—which means you can bet *everything* about that first Easter week was preordained, from the placement of the cross to the borrowed tomb.

So don't you think it's incredibly cool that God *chose* Mary Magdalene—this woman who'd been totally oppressed and completely marginalized—for what is arguably the most important job in biblical history? To be the first witness of the Resurrection, the very first human to testify that Jesus *had come back to life*! I know I do. Because it encourages me that He can use anybody—*any hot mess out there, including me!*—to tell the story of His Son and change the world. He can take someone totally dominated by the enemy and transform them into someone totally dominated by the Gospel! Thank You, Lord!

- **IF YOU WERE** writing the story, who would've been the hero/heroine that first Easter morning besides Mary from Fishville?

- **WHO'S THE MOST** unlikely missionary you've ever met?

- **HOW DOES MARY'S** story encourage you in your own evangelistic efforts?

Day 95
LOVING MORE PEOPLE, MORE

While Jesus was having dinner at Matthew's house, many tax collectors and sinners came and ate with him and his disciples. When the Pharisees saw this, they asked his disciples, "Why does your teacher eat with tax collectors and sinners?" On hearing this, Jesus said, "It is not the healthy who need a doctor, but the sick. But go and learn what this means: 'I desire mercy, not sacrifice.' For I have not come to call the righteous, but sinners." MATTHEW 9:10–13 NIV

YOU'VE PROBABLY HEARD THE old adage, *you can't teach an old dog new tricks.* Well I beg to differ. I can identify with the first part of that statement—especially in light of the proliferation of AARP ads jamming my mailbox the past few years—but I disagree with the inability to learn new stuff part because I've learned at least one new thing *every single day* since I brought Missy home from Haiti.

Besides having a brave warrior spirit and the predisposition to wiggle gleefully in the grocery store and greet bemused nearby shoppers with the impish invitation to dance with us (that's another new thing I've learned—dancing like nobody's watching in public places!), my little girl also has, as you know by now, HIV. Partly because of Missy's medical condition, but mostly because of her joyful exuberance, I'm learning to love more people, *more.*

One of my sweetest tutoring sessions took place right after I brought her home from Haiti, in the private pharmacy we now visit monthly that specializes in medication for people with HIV and AIDS. They don't sell candy, cards, breakfast cereal, toothpaste or Chia pets. Just pricey medicine. It's tucked away on the fifth floor of an old building that used to house a low-budget shopping mall. While coming and going from there, Missy and I have chatted it up with a few scantily-clad ladies of the evening, several rough-looking ex-cons, a transvestite in towering red heels, and lots of men in the latter stages of AIDS. The first two groups I was familiar with because of the time I've spent volunteering at an addiction recovery program, but I'd never spent any time around gaunt men with dark circles under their eyes and Kaposi's sarcoma (cancerous dermatological lesions that often accompany late-stage AIDS). That is, until God lavished me with the undeserved gift of becoming Missy's second mama.

Most of the other customers glanced at us with curiosity back then, probably because Missy was so tiny and was usually wearing a bow as big as her head and a plaid school uniform. They probably assumed we were lost, thinking surely this darling kid and her pale chaperon weren't going to the "special" pharmacy. But one day a man we were sharing the elevator with on the way to get her meds literally averted his gaze and exhaled in protest when Missy blurted out happily, "Hello Sur! How awe you?" I put my hand protectively on her shoulder and tried to stealthily scoot her a few inches away from him because he looked disheveled, had multiple sarcomas, and reeked of anger. But this was one of those times when her enthusiasm was not easily redirected. She tugged on his sleeve and persisted with more animation and volume, "I'm Missy Haar-Purr, SUR, and I'm FIVE! And this is my MAMA Haar-Purr!"

He threw me a look of frustration and exhaled louder, emphasizing his irritation at our presence. It was all I could do not to grin at his surprised expression when we walked into the pharmacy behind him and the darling women who run the place swarmed Missy like a bevy of favorite aunts. He seemed startled when they asked her to sing and she responded by belting out the praise chorus of "Your Great Name" followed by an enthusiastic, hip-swiveling encore of "Shake Your Booty" (Missy's musical repertoire is surprisingly vast). A few minutes later, after she'd proclaimed, "I lub ya'll!" and handed a big sucker to each staff member, she turned to him, held up her last remaining lollipop and asked sweetly, "Wood chu like a sucker, Sur?"

His expression softened as he leaned down and replied gently, "Well, yes honey . . . I believe I would." My daughter hugged him before bellowing a rather bossy "Goodbye Sur, it was nice to meed you!" At which point he reached over her head and shook my hand. When our eyes met, we both smiled. I couldn't speak because I was too close to tears. But I don't think we needed any more words. Enough had already been said.

- **WHO HAVE YOU** learned to love that you probably wouldn't have crossed paths with, or noticed if you did, five or ten years ago?

- **AND WHO WOULD** you say had to "learn" to love you?

- **WHY DO YOU** think we often back away from loving rough-and-tumble people the way Jesus did?

Day 96

THE COMEBACK KIDS

When they heard these things, they were enraged and gnashed their teeth at him. Stephen, full of the Holy Spirit, gazed into heaven. He saw the glory of God, and Jesus standing at the right hand of God. He said, "Look, I see the heavens opened and the Son of Man standing at the right hand of God!" They yelled at the top of their voices, covered their ears, and together rushed against him. They dragged him out of the city and began to stone him. And the witnesses laid their garments at the feet of a young man named Saul. While they were stoning Stephen, he called out, "Lord Jesus, receive my spirit!" He knelt down and cried out with a loud voice, "Lord, do not hold this sin against them!" And after saying this, he fell asleep. On that day a great persecution broke out against the church in Jerusalem, and all except the apostles were scattered throughout Judea and Samaria. . . . And those who had been scattered preached the word wherever they went. ACTS 7:54–8:1, 4 NIV

STEPHEN, LIKELY A RELATIVELY new Christ-follower, was also one of seven men the apostles had chosen to manage and allocate the charitable giving situation going on in Acts 7. Why? Because there'd been some fussing about how some of the needy folks were getting more financial assistance than others, so the apostles chose a few good men (which many congregations now refer to as deacons) to sort it all out (Acts 6:1–4).

Therefore, it stands to reason that Stephen, being a chosen member of the very first deaconate, was a wise, honorable, well-liked kind of guy. He was probably on the school board and raised money for the March of Dimes, too. And we know for sure that he was passionate about the Gospel because Luke literally describes him as: *a man with great faith and full of the Holy Spirit* (Acts 6:5b). So it's not hard to imagine the collective shock and grief that rippled through that fledgling church community when he was stoned to death by a militant, anti-Christian mob simply because of one straightforward sermon about their generational stubborn streak and desperate need for Jesus.

Humanly speaking, it would've made sense for the early church to recoil after the tragedy of their dear friend's gruesome murder and then retreat. It'd make sense if they chose to circle their proverbial wagons and focus on consoling the core group of their fellowship. Maybe hire a grief counselor, a crisis manager, and some administrative help to wade through all the insurance and liability issues. But they didn't shrink back in fear. They didn't go underground and become a secret, self-protective, cultish kind of crew. They didn't allow a horrific homicide to curb their cause. Nope. They did the exact opposite. Their commitment to love others for the sake of Christ didn't get buried with Stephen—it rose up and got bigger! The enemy's knock-out punch didn't send them reeling to the canvas—it propelled them to the witnessing *Olympics*!

Here's the ironic thing about hardship. It tends to have the reverse effect on those of us who've put our hope in Jesus instead of our circumstances. Instead of staying down when we're walloped, God's people tend to bounce back with more oomph. In fact, church history proves that opposition often works like Miracle Gro on the body of Christ. The power of the Holy Spirit enables us to have Rocky-like comebacks, pointing to the undefeatable, redemptive power of the Gospel. We may be down, but we're never out!

- **WHEN HAVE YOU** been tempted to throw in the towel when it comes to sharing the love of Christ with unreceptive—maybe even antagonistic—people in your life?

- **HOW HAVE YOU** seen God use a tragic situation to mobilize His church for good purposes?

- **WHEN YOU FEEL** the urge to recoil and retreat in the face of hardship, how can you tap back into God's great power to help you bounce back?

Day 97

THE SUN WILL COME UP, TOMORROW

For his anger lasts only a moment,
but his favor, a lifetime.
Weeping may stay overnight,
but there is joy in the morning. PSALM 30:5

WHEN I REALLY BEGAN dealing with—and honestly *feeling*—the trauma of my childhood, I was inspired to be more candid about my struggles and drop my happy mask after reading how C. S. Lewis struggled with debilitating sadness and questioned God's goodness after losing his wife, Joy, to cancer. As I matured emotionally, I delved even further into the relationship between happiness and hardship—which are often woven together, I've found. This exploration led me to study the life of prolific pastor Charles Haddon Spurgeon who battled with severe depression.

Despite the fact that twenty-five thousand people bought copies of his sermons every week at the height of his ministry, and he got to preach to ten million people before his death in 1892, Spurgeon still had days when he didn't want to get out of bed. Following one of his darkest moments he said, "There are dungeons beneath the castles of despair."[19]

Now that I'm well past the normal midpoint of life and have surely lived more years than there are years left in my story, I've come to the firm belief that no one gets out of life without at least a little pain and anguish. Show me an adult who says they haven't, and they're either a fibber, mentally unbalanced, or have amnesia.

I'm so grateful God gives us time and space and emotions capable of processing dark nights of the soul, and I'm equally thankful that the Gospel frees us from pretending everything's awesome when it's not. But I'm even more glad that He gave us the mental faculties to ultimately recover our joy regardless of whether it was illegitimately hijacked or overshadowed by legitimate grief. The following passages, as it turns out, agree with the scientific research out there on happiness; namely, that our minds really do have the power to correct negative, destructive thought patterns:

Do not conform to the pattern of this world, but be transformed by the renewing of your mind. Then you will be able to test and approve what God's will is—his good, pleasing and perfect will. (Rom. 12:2 NIV)

"Who has known the mind of the Lord? Who has been able to teach him? But we have the mind of Christ." (1 Cor. 2:16 NCV)

For God has not given us a spirit of fear, but of power and of love and of a sound mind. (2 Tim. 1:7 NKJV)

In other words, with the Holy Spirit's help, you and I have the power to kick "stinkin' thinkin'" to the curb and recapture hope, happiness, and peace! This doesn't mean we have to ignore hardship or dark situations. It simply means we don't have to be *ruled* by those things. Joy is a legitimate posture we have the Spirit's power to reclaim!

- **WHAT SPIRITUAL HABITS** have you discovered that best help renew your mind and rekindle your joy?

- **HOW HAVE YOU** seen God weave together hardship and joy in your life?

- **WHY DO YOU** think you sometimes resist the call to choose joy in your thought-life?

Day 98
THROUGH THICK AND THIN

Then Job answered:
I have heard many things like these.
You are all miserable comforters.
Is there no end to your empty words?
What provokes you that you continue testifying?
If you were in my place I could also talk like you.
I could string words together against you
and shake my head at you.
Instead, I would encourage you with my mouth,
and the consolation from my lips would bring relief. JOB 16:1–5

WHILE I WAS IN the process of adopting Missy, a dear friend (who's also the adoptive mom of an HIV+ child they got to bring home several years before I began our journey) soberly warned me about disingenuous religious people. She said, "Be careful about throwing the pearl of your and Missy's relationship before the swine of Southern facades. Most of the women you know from church will praise you initially for being such a 'good' person and rescuing a baby from certain death in a Third World country. They'll throw all kinds of accolades in your direction. But just wait until you actually bring Missy home and she goes from being a picture on their refrigerator to being a real-live student in the same classroom as their children. Your Christian friends' real feelings will come out when they choose whether or not to invite your beautiful little girl to their kid's pool party."

I didn't really know how to respond to her unvarnished candor and wondered if maybe she'd developed a root of bitterness over one bad apple of a mom who was less-than-gracious after they brought their baby home.

But then a few months after Missy came home, we bumped into another mother and her daughter—whom I've known for years from church circles—at Costco. After a polite greeting where we introduced our suddenly shy daughters, who are exactly the same age, I watched that mama's eyes shift and break contact with mine as her countenance hardened into a fake smile. Then I listened in sad dismay while her voice rose into a perky falsetto as she prattled something along the lines of, "When my schedule isn't so crazy maybe we can get our girls together sometime for a play date!" all the while sticking her arm out like a human guardrail then slowly sweeping her baby girl backwards, away from Missy. And then my straightforward friend's cautionary advice came rushing back to me like last night's bean and cheese burrito!

Which, if you've ever read the book of Job, sounds a lot like his experience with his pretend friends, too:

> *You are all miserable comforters...* in other words, you cover up your true feelings with dishonest prattling and your fake compassion is utterly useless in easing my pain!

> *Is there no end to your empty words?...* in other words, the spiritual platitudes you've been quoting to me are as useless and temporal as the ash at the bottom of our fireplace or the gum on the bottom of my boot!

> *What provokes you that you should continue testifying?...* in other words, please shut your trap because every hokey, disingenuous word that falls out of your big mouth is landing on my last nerve!

Now, I know what you're thinking—*who's the one with the root of bitterness, now?* Let me admit to the fact that yes, that encounter really did pierce me to the core. The false self I saw in that mom made me want to scream. But it also caused me to ponder all my own false moments, and truth be told, as I look back at my past in certain seasons, I'm just as guilty of fakeness in my friendships.

I deeply regret having presented a false self for years to friends and family members, many of whom were emotionally mature and secure enough to love me well—warts and all—yet couldn't access a *real* relationship with me because of my own strong stiff-arm of pretense holding them at a "safe" distance. Which is one of the reasons I'm both encouraged and convicted by Job's pleas for his friends to be more authentic. He was right to call them on all the inauthenticity, just as God is right to call us on ours. Fake is no way to live when it comes to the kind of friendships God wants us to have.

- **PROVERBS 17:17 SAYS,** "A friend loves at all times, and a brother is born for a difficult time." Who fits that description in your life?

- **IN WHICH OF** your friendships do you tend to put on a mask? Why?

- **HOW MIGHT YOU** be a more authentic person and friend to those around you? Where do you need to be more authentic with God Himself?

Day 99
HIDDEN TREASURE

"I have told you these things so that in me you may have peace. You will have suffering in this world. Be courageous! I have conquered the world." JOHN 16:33

AT THE END OF my freshman year in high school, my stepfather gave me a choice. He said if I chose to stay at Lake Brantley High School, I would no longer be allowed to participate in extra-curricular activities like student government, social clubs, or sports because he was the principal at the middle school next door, and he wanted me to drive home with him as soon as he got off work. He was not willing to wait around for me to be finished with track practice or an FCA meeting, and he flatly refused to drive twenty-five miles round trip to pick me up from anything sports or social-related after hours.

However, he bargained, if I agreed to transfer to Seminole High School, the secondary school in our town, I could participate in whatever clubs or sports I wanted to because it was close enough for me to ride my bike to and from activities. Mom tried to change his mind because after we met with a much-less-than hospitable staff member at Seminole (whose grammar was even more atrocious than his lack of civility), she became concerned about their lackluster academic standards, not to mention the rampant drug use, racial tension, and campus violence that was often reported in the local news. Despite the fact that mom graduated from Seminole High School and had met Dad Angel there thirty years earlier, she was more concerned about my safety and college preparation than she was nostalgic about me attending her Alma Mater.

But Dad Angel wouldn't budge. So I left all my friends and a sparkling clean, recently built school with a bevy of amenities to attend a very old school with ramshackle buildings, zero modern amenities, and a constant police presence in August of 1978. The first few days were definitely dicey—I got chased more than once by a gang leader who wanted to rough me up to bolster his reputation as the number one bully; a girl hurled an expletive at me and threatened to beat me up because her boyfriend gave me directions to the Driver's Ed class when he noticed I was lost, and my preppy clothes made me a laughingstock at the lockers between classes.

But soon enough, I befriended the bully after his sister told him we were friends in elementary school, learned to avoid boys who were attached to mean, possessive girls prone to wearing tube tops in public, and exchanged khakis and top-siders for Levi's and flip-flops.

More important, I learned to love people who didn't look like me or live in my neighborhood. I learned that skin color and zip codes and bank accounts and test scores were petty details and absolutely useless qualifiers for real relationships. I learned to make do with hand-me-down uniforms, generously cracked tennis courts, sagging nets, and a gym without air-conditioning in the intense heat and sticky humidity of Central Florida. I learned how to ask better questions in class and check out more books from the library. I learned how to engage in dialogue instead of distancing through diatribe. I learned how to gladly share microscopes and dissecting equipment in an antiquated laboratory under the guidance of an awesome anatomy teacher. I learned how to be a team player and cheer even louder from the bench than I did on the court.

Seminole High School is where I learned that entitlement is the archenemy of creativity, passion, and joy. It's where I learned that building something by the sweat of your brow is a lot more rewarding than having it handed to you. It's where I learned to lead Bible studies with my best friend Cindy. It's where we first studied the theme of adoption in the Bible. It's where we made a solemn promise before an FCA meeting that we'd adopt hard-to-place kids when we grew up. Which means it's also where I unwittingly began the journey of becoming Missy's mama, thirty years before her first mama died in a small village in Haiti.

I couldn't have known at the time, but my Dad Angel's ultimatum was a tool in the hands of God to teach me some things that are hard to learn in a perfectly pristine classroom. What I thought was a trial ended up being a treasure.

- **HOW HAS A** trial recently resulted in unexpected treasure in your life?

- **IF YOU ARE** in a situation you wouldn't have chosen for yourself, what are some things you are learning along the way?

- **WHAT MIGHT GOD** be using this trial to prepare you for?

Day 100
SEW JOY

Rejoice in the Lord always. I will say it again: Rejoice! Let your graciousness be known to everyone. PHILIPPIANS 4:4–5

A FEW YEARS AGO I had the privilege of going to Thessaloniki, Greece, for the second time with my dear friend, Christine Caine, along with several of my closest friends from Nashville to introduce them to A21, the incredibly effective anti-human-trafficking organization that Chris founded with her husband, Nick. What none of us knew while planning the trip was that the greatest refugee crisis since World War II would be taking place just a few hours from our hotel in Greece as hundreds (and sometimes thousands) of mostly Syrian men, women, and children fleeing their country's violent war and the cruel oppression of ISIS extremists were washing up on the shores of the Greek island of Lesbos every single day because of its proximity to Turkey and Syria on the northern shore of the Aegean Sea.

Which is why we volunteered when we heard the UN was desperate for volunteers to help with the unprecedented influx of refugees. Most of these refugees fled their homes with only the clothes on their backs and had lost loved ones on their perilous journey across the Aegean because merciless pirates often crammed over one hundred passengers (all of whom were charged exorbitant "transport" fees) onto inflatable life rafts suitable for no more than twenty so as to increase their profits. As you can imagine, many drowned in their frantic quest for asylum. So we unanimously agreed to pile into vans and drive several hours to a remote, abandoned train station—one that had hurriedly been turned into a tent city serving as the second official stop for refugees after being processed by the Greek government at Lesbos.

I don't have words to adequately describe the hopelessness of the first group of refugees we watched climb out of buses a few hundred yards away from where UN officials asked my friends and me to help assess each individual or family's most urgent needs and then direct them to the corresponding tent. We were quickly overwhelmed by a crush of people begging for help. And in short order we amended the slow and ineffective "sorting system" and began passing out food rations to everyone within reach, giving all the parents bouncing infants on their hips formula for their starving babies, and teasing with a rag-tag crew of rambunctious, teenage boys who were hungry for some small sense of normalcy amidst the trauma and sensed that a group of bossy female volunteers from America might be just the place to find it.

Yet by far the most effective "aid" we handed out during those October evenings happened when we got transferred to the juvenile tent, where hundreds of beautiful but apprehensive kids were gathered, flanked by their worried mamas and daddies. Men and women who felt they had no choice but to leave behind their war-ravaged homeland and militant jihadists, yet knowing that what their children had witnessed in the pursuit of safety and a better way of life may well have caused permanent emotional damage.

Since there were no video games or toys to entertain those darling kids with, and because none of us could speak any of the Middle Eastern dialects represented, we began singing and dancing a very animated version of the Hokey Pokey as a last resort. Unbeknownst to us, the Hokey Pokey is a universal favorite, and almost immediately the refugee children formed a giant circle with the "crazy American chicks" and began singing and dancing their little hearts out, too.

And we just might have set a Guinness Book world record dancing the Hokey Pokey there on the frigid border of Greece and Macedonia because those precious peanuts were tireless! Whenever one of us stopped to catch our breath, they'd pull on our sleeves and plead for us to keep on going in lilting accents we couldn't understand, but with adorable upturned faces that were impossible to refuse.

At one point, I stepped out of the cacophonous ring of hokey-pokiers to take off my heavy sweatshirt and a young Muslim mom in a full burka approached shyly and asked, "May I speak with you for a moment?" in perfect English. I said, "Yes, of course." And was then completely caught off guard when she took my hands in hers, looked into my eyes, and said with a quiet smile, "Thank you so much for dancing with my son. His little sister was killed a few weeks before we left Syria and he's been despondent ever since. This is the first time I've seen him laugh in a long time. My husband and I are so grateful to you."

She continued by saying she knew we were Christians and she believed our prayers to be powerful. Then she humbly asked if I would mind praying for her son's joy to return. I told her I'd be honored and asked if I could have her permission to invoke the name of Jesus while I prayed for him. She considered my request solemnly for a few seconds before nodding graciously. I've prayed hundreds of thousands, if not millions, of prayers in my lifetime but few have felt more sacred than when I got to hold Farema's hand and pray for Jesus to mend her little boy's broken heart.

I've never forgotten that experience—how Jesus can use one song and dance to spread joy, and spread His *name*, even in the worst of circumstances. The unconditional love of our Creator Redeemer brings tangible hope, lasting peace, and supernatural resurrection power that can restore what death tries to steal. *Wouldn't it be awesome if there was a Spirited gang of obsessively grateful, undone by Jesus, genuinely happy and not faking it through the hard stuff kind of believers, who were willing to run headlong into real life bellowing this glorious good news of the Gospel?* I'm absolutely convinced it would change the world . . . at least our little corner of it!

- **WOULD THE PEOPLE** who know you best describe your joy as "contagious"?

- **WHY DO YOU** think you sometimes shy away from sharing the joy of Christ in your spheres of influence?

- **WHERE COULD YOU** stand to sew just a little bit more joy in Jesus' name?

NOTES

1. www.dictionary.com

2. Randy Alcorn, *Happiness* (Downer's Grove, IL: Tyndale Publishers, 2015), 19.

3. Tremper Longman III, *How to Read the Psalms* (Downer's Grove, IL: InterVarsity, 1988), 45.

4. Spiro Zodhiates, ed., *Hebrew-Greek Key Word Study Bible* (Chattanooga, TN: AMG, 1996), 627, 1911.

5. *Strong's Concordance Greek #3107: mákarios*, "happy"; https://biblehub.com/greek/3107.htm.

6. Sonja Lyubomirsky, *The How of Happiness: A Scientific Approach to Getting the Life You Want* (New York: Penguin Books, 2007), 20–23.

7. C. S. Lewis, *The Problem of Pain* (New York: HarperOne, 1940), 92.

8. Lesslie Newbigin, *The Gospel in a Pluralistic Society* (London: SPCK, 1989), 227.

9. Henri Nouwen, *The Wounded Healer* (New York: Doubleday, 1971), 66.

10. Charles Spurgeon, *The New Park Street Pulpit: The Immutability of God* (delivered on January 7, 1855 at New Park Street Chapel, Southwark, UK).

11. Elie Wiesel (the author of "Night" and winner of the 1986 Nobel Peace Prize) as quoted in 1986 an interview with *U.S. News & World Report* magazine.

12. Tim Keller, *King's Cross* (New York: Dutton, 2011), 86.

13. C. S. Lewis, *Mere Christianity* (New York: HarperCollins Publishers, 1952), 60.

14. Donald Spoto, *Reluctant Saint* (New York: Penguin, 2003).

15. Marcus Braybrooke, *Beacons of the Light: 100 Holy People Who Have Shaped the History of Humanity* (New Alresford, UK: John Hunt Publishing, 2009), 287.

16. C. S. Lewis, *The Four Loves* (New York: Harcourt Brace, 1960), 155.

17. Timothy Keller, *Counterfeit Gods* (New York: Penguin Books, 2011), 3.

18. Edward T. Welch, *Addictions: A Banquet in the Grave* (Phillipsburg, NJ: P&R Publishing House, 2001), xvi.

19. Arnold Dallimore, *Spurgeon: A New Biography* (Edinburgh, UK: Banner of Truth, 1987), 186.

Check out some of Lisa's other great books!

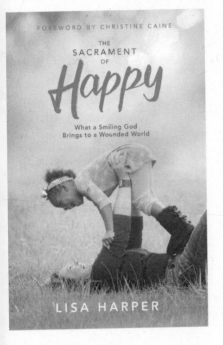

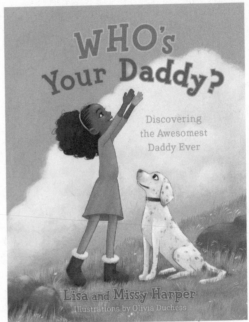

THE SACRAMENT OF HAPPY

Many think happiness is circumstantially-based, therefore "unspiritual", so it's a delight to tag along with Lisa as she dives deep into Scripture to prove otherwise!

WHO'S YOUR DADDY?

When someone asks Missy a big question—"Who's your daddy?"—she starts thinking and learning a lot about daddies, especially Daddy God, who loves us all unconditionally.